Historic
MOVIE THEATERS
—— of ——
DELAWARE

MICHAEL J. NAZAREWYCZ

Published by The History Press
Charleston, SC
www.historypress.com

Copyright © 2019 by Michael J. Nazarewycz
All rights reserved

Front cover, top, left to right: Ball Theatre, 214 Main Street, Millsboro, circa 1958. *Photo by Robert F. Ferrier, courtesy of the Town of Millsboro*; an original spool of Reese Theatre tickets, circa 1960. *Photo by Victoria Nazarewycz*; the Temple Theatre in Dover. *Delaware Public Archives, Dover, Delaware*; *bottom*: the Warner Theatre, Wilmington. *Delaware Public Archives, Dover, Delaware.* *Back cover, top, left to right*: The marquee at the Clayton Theatre, 2017. *Photo by Victoria Nazarewycz*; DelMar Drive-In, undated. *Delaware Public Archives, Dover, Delaware*; this artist's rendition of the opening night at the Warner Theatre, complete with accurate marquee and framed by the Warner Bros. shield, was featured on the cover of the theater's opening night program in 1939. *Delaware Public Archives, Dover, Delaware*; *bottom*: The Everett Theatre was used for both interior and exterior scenes in Peter Weir's *Dead Poets Society*. *Courtesy of the Everett Theatre.*

First published 2019

Manufactured in the United States

ISBN 9781625858474

Library of Congress Control Number: 2018960971

Notice: The information in this book is true and complete to the best of our knowledge. It is offered without guarantee on the part of the author or The History Press. The author and The History Press disclaim all liability in connection with the use of this book.

All rights reserved. No part of this book may be reproduced or transmitted in any form whatsoever without prior written permission from the publisher except in the case of brief quotations embodied in critical articles and reviews.

*This book is dedicated to my wife, Judy;
to my daughters, Victoria and Veronica;
and to my late grandmother, Irena.*

CONTENTS

Preface 7
Acknowledgements 11
Introduction 13

[Take 1] The First Theater: There Can Be Only One 15

[Take 2] The Nineteenth Century:
       The (Opera) Housing Boom 19

[Take 3] The Early Twentieth Century: Pictures, Moving 30

[Take 4] The 1910s: The Rising South 42

[Take 5] The 1920s: Volume 61

[Take 6] The 1930s: Slower, Lower 76

[Take 7] The 1940s: Powers, Allied 89

[Take 8] The 1950s: (Close) Out with the Old,
       (Drive) In with the New 113

[Take 9] The 1960s: Equality for All, Immorality for Some 129

CONTENTS

[Take 10] The 1970s: Of Movies, Sex and the Multiplex   143

[Take 11] The 1980s: The Decade of Downsizing   160

[Take 12] The 1990s: The Meh Decade   174

[Take 13] The New Millennium: Yesterday, Today
    and Tomorrow   182

Roll Credits   195

Sources   205
About the Author   208

PREFACE

One of my favorite film quotes is "Life finds a way."
The statement, as spoken by Dr. Ian Malcolm (Jeff Goldblum) in Steven Spielberg's *Jurassic Park*, is made in the context of evolution—that no matter what constraints man puts on nature and, at a higher level, Life itself, Life will always find a way to proceed the way it thinks it should. It's a line I've often used to explain fate or fateful happenings. Events occur the way they occur because Life wants the order it wants. Such is the case with this book.

I had been writing film reviews and film-related commentary for several years, and as much as I loved doing it, I was ready for something more. I wanted to stay within the realm of film, albeit less critical, and I wanted it long form. I was basically itching to write a book. I flirted with several ideas, and while I liked them all, none would work for various reasons. As I awaited further inspiration, the website I was writing reviews for went dark. Suddenly, I had more free time on my hands.

Life began finding its way.

Meanwhile, things at my day job were taking their toll, and the sense of defeat I felt coming home every evening, coupled with the loss of the strict schedule I had writing film reviews, left me using my idle evenings for little more than mental decompression and a steady diet of mindless screen time. One night, though, mindless screen time met inspiration. In my Facebook feed, I came across an item that got me thinking about how all the old movie theaters from my youth were gone and had been for years. How did this happen? How did I miss it? That gave me the idea to write something nostalgic about the glory days of my moviegoing youth. I found my project.

Life continued to forge its path.

This nostalgia book filled my evenings with greater purpose and made my days more bearable, but Life wasn't finished yet. My daytime professional circumstances improved, and a renewed sense of self-worth in the day changed my demeanor at night. I found myself with the energy I needed to attack the project with vigor.

Life still wasn't done.

As I performed preliminary research on the theaters of my youth, as well as other theaters that were open in my lifetime but I had never gotten the chance to visit, I found stories—quirky stories and unique stories and stories you might never have heard. I learned the place where I had seen my first in-theater, live-action movie at about the age of six was the first twin cinema in Delaware. I uncovered a story about the night when a Hollywood A-lister planned to slip into a different theater, one that became a cinematic haunt in my life, to test-screen his latest picture. I discovered a drive-in from my youth was supposed to close one summer but lived for one more season because of red tape. The stories continued to mount, and they all had something in common: they weren't stories about me and my experiences there, they were stories about the theaters, stories I never knew, even though those stories were happening right in front of me. And they were stories that had been recorded but hadn't really been told—at least not as a collective. With every new discovery I made, I knew this was the book that needed to be written—not a book about me at these theaters, but a book about these theaters as told by me.

Life found its way.

Life found its scope, too. What began as a look into the theaters of my youth grew into an investigation into the theaters of New Castle County, which exploded into a long and deep dive into almost every theatrical entity in the state's history that at some point showed movies to customers. I say "almost" because, for as exhaustive an attempt at completionism as this has been, I know I don't have them all. Surely some small town had some small theater that existed for some small length of time and I just never learned about it. Over the course of my twenty months tackling this glorious beast, I happened across stray names and random mentions of places I either found little to nothing more about or places I was unable to confirm had shown movies. I give them mentions throughout this book, hoping maybe those mentions will spur the discovery of more history about them elsewhere.

Preface

But what do I mean by *theatrical entity*? As time passes, some theaters change owners, names, their number of screens or even their addresses. As my list began to take shape and I charted the evolution of some theaters, I decided to count each place as a theatrical entity, not necessarily as an individual theater.

For example, if a theater like the Naamans Drive-In or the Clayton Theatre only ever existed in one location, under one name, I counted that as one theatrical entity. If a theater, over the course of its life, existed in a single location but had multiple names—like the Royal Theatre, which would become the Elaine Theatre, the Colonial Theatre and finally end its time as the Earle Theatre—I counted that not as four theaters, but as one theatrical entity.

In a few cases, a theatrical entity not only changed names but also changed locations, like when its owner decided to close one place and open a new place somewhere else *to replace it*. This was the case when the owner of Wilmington's Comedy Theatre closed shop and opened Hyrup's Auditorium a short walk up Market Street. The Auditorium later became the Red Moon Motion Picture Theatre and then the Gem Theatre before finally closing as the Comique Picture Palace. Five shingles. Two addresses. One theatrical entity.

Finally, there are cases in which a theatrical entity remained in one place but had multiple names, multiple owners and/or may have had gaps when it was closed and later reopened. The most recent example of this is the Cinema Center, which opened, changed hands several times and closed, only to be sold again, razed, rebuilt, renamed and reopened as Main Street Movies 5. Two shingles, at least four owners, two buildings, one location and a one-year gap in its existence? One theatrical entity.

There are two additional notes in reference to theatrical entities and breaks in their timelines. First, when you see the initial appearance of each entity throughout this book, you will see the occasional asterisk next to the name(s) the theater went by. The purpose of the asterisk is to call out a break in time when the theater was closed and later reopened under a different name. For example, the Smyrna Opera House closed in 1923 and opened again as the Como Theatre in 1931. You will find an asterisk there (*Smyrna Opera House | 1870–circa 1923**). If a theater closed and later reopened under the same name, you will see the timeline break but no asterisk (*Reese Theatre | 1922–1943, 1945–1966*).

Second is how I have chosen to define timeline breaks. My original intent was to be strict and cite all documented theater closures regardless of length of time. That quickly became difficult to manage, as some closures were very brief and not thoroughly reported. I then decided to equate a closure to one year, but even that was difficult to track. I settled on what I think is a good rule: if a theater was closed (regardless of reason) for an entire *calendar* year, I considered that a recordable timeline break. The Everett, for example, closed at least five times in its history, but only twice did closures span the entirety of a full calendar year. The thinking here is that if a theater was open in any given part of a year, I counted that year as a whole.

As you read the stories of Delaware's movie houses and multiplexes, keep in mind that as part of a greater theatrical entity, the theater you knew may have been called something else before you knew it. Be patient. Travel through time. You may remember your theater as the Rialto, but first you'll live through it as the Lyric. But *your* theater will eventually appear. And maybe, just maybe, you will see it again for the first time.

ACKNOWLEDGEMENTS

Historical Organizations

Air Mobility Command Museum: Michael D. Leister
Duck Creek Historical Society; Smyrna Museum: Jess Hansen
Felton Community Historical Society: Sarah Ferguson
Fort Miles Historical Association: Dr. Gary Wray
Georgetown Historical Society; Seaford Historical Society: Jim Bowden
Greater Harrington Historical Society: Viva Poore, Doug Poore
Laurel Historical Society: Ned and Norma Jean Fowler
Lewes Historical Society: Mike DiPaolo
Middletown Historical Society: Alison Matsen, Christopher Collins
Milford Museum: Claudia Furnish Leister, Barbara Jones
Milton Historical Society: Kimberly Fabbri, PhD
Newark Historical Society: Mary Torbey
New Castle Historical Society: Susan Hannell
Rehoboth Beach Historical Society; Rehoboth Beach Museum: Nancy Alexander
Town of Bethany Beach Cultural and Historical Affairs: Carol Olmstead
University of Delaware Library, Manuscripts and Archives Department: Jaime Margalotti

Theaters

Cinema Art Theater: Sue Early
Clayton Theatre: Joanne Howe

Acknowledgements

Everett Theatre: Christopher Everett
Milton Theatre: JP Lecap
Movies at Midway: Richard Derrickson, Tiffany Derrickson
Penn Cinema Riverfront: Penn Ketchum
Riverfront Theater: Joe-Anne Corwin, Tracy Dissinger
Smyrna Opera House: Donna Cantillon, Emily Cummings
Theatre N: Bob Weir
Trabant University Center Theatre: Andrea Boyle, Cheryl Cunningham

Other Organizations

Archives of the Catholic Diocese of Wilmington: Susan Kirk Ryan
Delaware Public Archives: Randy Goss
Delaware State Parks; Fort DuPont State Park; Port Penn Interpretive Center: Jake Miller
Greenwood Public Library: Catharine Kramer
Painted Stave Distilling: Mike Rasmussen, Ron Gomes
Roman Theater Management: Rick Roman
Town of Millsboro: Matt Hall

Individuals

Tim Ayers
Amy (Ayers) Higgins
Sue Bramhall
Joanne Christian
Howard Dickerson
Albert Franklin
JJ Garvine
Mark L. Lawlor
Kendall Messick
Victoria Nazarewycz
Fritz Schranck

The History Press

Abigail Fleming
Banks Smither

INTRODUCTION

On December 7, 1787, Delaware became the first state to ratify the U.S. Constitution. Some 214 years later, House Bill #395 was approved by Delaware's General Assembly. That bill formally made the official nickname of Delaware "The First State." Although the nickname became official in recent history, it has carried semi-official heft for decades, having been added to the state's license plates in 1962.

Being the first state to ratify the Constitution was a definitive first. There is no room for parsing anything. Someone had to ratify it first, Delaware did it, and from that day forward, no other state could make that claim. (Sorry, Pennsylvania.) As I wrote this book, with history as both my subject and my inspiration, I had hoped that determining the first theater in Delaware would have been equally as definitive.

Not even close. Defining which theater should be the first theater in Delaware became an exercise not unlike the lies, damned lies, and statistics of Hollywood box office numbers. Yes, there is one film that is the highest grossing film of a given year, but to help sell Blu-rays, a studio will quickly deem some other film the highest domestic grossing PG-13 horror film of all time (not adjusted for inflation). Who needs definitive when you have fancy?

I fell into this trap, or rather, I gained a better understanding of the importance of shaping a narrative. So, because theaters existed before film, ergo film was introduced to theaters, my search for the first theater began with all theaters.

Introduction

I went back to the first days of entertainment in the state, just a few years after that historic ratification, when in 1798, English comedian John Bernard led an operatic group through a series of statewide appearances. I ruled out that first, as it was not an actual theater. I also ruled out what appears to be the first formal theater in the state: a Wilmington building at the corner of Sixth and Shipley Streets built in 1834 by the Wilmington Theatre Company and used by it until 1839. Sure, it may have been the first physical theater, but the place was gone not long after it had started, and gone with still decades to go until film showed up on the timeline (and no films ever subsequently screened at that physical address, to the best of my knowledge).

I reconsidered my approach and tried to determine when the first film screened in the state, thus establishing the theater where it played as the first theater in the state. This was difficult, as early pioneers in film exhibition weren't necessarily associated with theaters. Exhibitioners took their show on the road to halls, churches and even parks. Also, many theaters played collections of short reels with their usual vaudeville offerings. These hodgepodge screenings were reported in papers as news items, but I cannot determine how thorough that reporting was to establish that first.

So I decided the first theater should be identified as the first theater built that would go on to show movies at some point in its history. The Queen, at Fifth and Market Streets in Wilmington, looked like it fit that bill, having been built in 1789 and having shown movies for more than forty years, starting in 1916, but I ruled it out. While the Queen existed in the first building to house a theater that showed movies, it wasn't the first theater; it was built as a hotel, thus not the first place constructed for the purposes of entertainment (read: theater) that would go on to show movies as part of its greater entertainment repertoire.

Like I said, who needs definitive when you have fancy?

Ultimately, the first theater—that first place built to entertain people and then later show films—would not be built in Wilmington, the state's eventual theater epicenter. That first theater would be built about thirty miles south, and not until almost eighty years after the opening of the Indian Queen Hotel.

TAKE 1

THE FIRST THEATER

There Can Be Only One

FADE IN

Seven years before the first theater would become a reality, that theater's town would first become incorporated. But even before that—hundreds of years before that—the town would first come to be.

Middletown, named as such for its location about halfway between Appoquinimink Creek (in Odessa) and Bohemia Landing (on the Bohemia River in Maryland), was originally home to the Lenni-Lenape tribe and was later settled by Europeans in the late 1600s. As milling and farming grew, so too did the town, and by the mid-1800s, the Delaware Railroad had completed construction, making Middletown a town of considerable convenience. Add to that its desirable crops of wheat, corn and peaches, and Middletown found itself ripe for incorporation. On February 12, 1861, the Delaware General Assembly made that incorporation so.

When the first town council decided the town should be one mile square, Middletown became known as the "Diamond Town of the Diamond State." Little did anyone know that just a few years later, a place would open in town that would eventually go on to become the crown jewel of Middletown's arts, and Delaware's theater, history.

OPENING CREDITS

Middletown Opera House | 1868–1922
Everett Theatre | 1922–1932, 1934–1979, 1982–present
(Middletown)

Having already been unsuccessful in attempting to build a Masonic Temple for use by Union Lodge #5 A.F. & A.M. in 1853, the Middletown Hall Company was formed in 1866 with the purpose to build a town hall. On July 27, 1868, the cornerstone of that town hall was laid on West Main Street.

The morning-long rain on that Monday was unpromising, but the spirit of the occasion wouldn't be dampened. The ceremony of laying the cornerstone of the town hall, as conducted by the M.W. Grand Lodge of Delaware, had a strong attendance, with delegations representing Delaware Lodges from Wilmington, New Castle, Delaware City, Smyrna and Dover, as well as Maryland Lodges from Millington and Chesapeake City.

As chronicled by the then-fledgling *Middletown Transcript*, the 2:00 p.m. procession line was formed and "moved down Main Street to Catherine, countermarched to Broad, up Broad to Lake, down Lake to Wood, down Wood to Main, and thence to the Hall."

The Odessa Cornet Band provided the opening music, after which statements were delivered, a hymn was performed and a prayer by Reverend Mr. Crowle was offered to round out the opening. This was followed by a reading of the items contained in "The Box," something of a time capsule, to be placed in the cornerstone. Those items:

- Middletown Hall Company's history
- Names of Middletown Hall Company stockholders and officers
- Map of Middletown
- Middletown business directory
- Copies of the first issue of the *Middletown Transcript* and each of Wilmington's newspapers
- List of members of Union Lodge #5 A.F. & A.M.
- List of officers of the M.W. Grand Lodge of Delaware
- Various U.S. coins
- English farthing from 1775 found in the building that previously stood where town hall now did
- Continental, Confederate and U.S. paper money

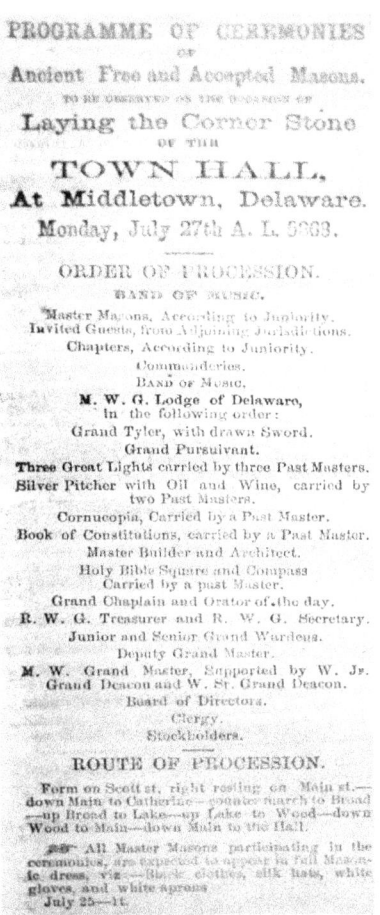

On a rainy Monday in 1868, the Middletown Town Hall cornerstone was laid (via the *Middletown Transcript*). *Middletown Historical Society.*

The remainder of the afternoon was filled with more presentations, prayers and hymns, and with the ceremonies complete, the town hall was formally ready for business. The three-story brick building, measuring 100 by 125 feet, would house on its third floor a trio of rooms to be utilized by the Union Lodge. On its first floor were town offices and retail space. And on the second floor, the first theater: the Middletown Opera House.

Also referred to as the Auditorium or Middletown Hall in its early decades, the Opera House provided the residents of the Diamond Town of the Diamond State a wide array of entertainment and other offerings in those early years, at a variety of prices. Some shows charged an admission of fifty cents for adults and half that for kids; others offered a thirty-five-/twenty-five-cent price point, with the higher amount for reserved seating; others still cost ten cents for one show or forty cents for a season pass. Regardless of price, audiences were fed a steady entertainment diet of local and imported flavors.

Local talent included students from the Middletown Academy performing a variety of acts, including dialogues, readings and music; residents of neighboring Townsend performed a dramatic play; and the Amphions, a musical act that, based on how they were promoted in advertisements, might well have been the nineteenth-century equivalent of a house band, routinely provided needed music. Among the imported entertainment were acts like Artemas Ward and his wax figures; Simmons and Slocum's Minstrels ("The Champion Troupe of America"); and Sanford's Opera Troupe, which boasted a program "more varied, more attractive, more original, more novel than that of any other troupe before the public."

The Opera House wasn't solely about form, though; it also served functionally as a venue for a diverse mix of community events, including lectures by Reverend John Collins McCabe ("Woman's Worth and Woman's Work" and "Woman's Rights and Woman's Wrongs" were two); temperance meetings (some with entertainment, some with large crowds, but all with the goal of "arresting the course of but one inebriate and saving the wreck of but one life"); and fundraisers for causes like the Volunteer Hose Company. Also set at the Opera House were moments of importance, at least for some locals. In 1891, commencement exercises for the Middletown Academy were held. On that night, five young men—Samuel Kelley, Thomas Kibbler, Reese Parker, Samuel Rothwell and Harry Tatman—moved on to their next level of education. They comprised the entire graduating class.

The Opera House also played host to political meetings. One such meeting brought together the Republicans of St. Georges and the Young Men's Republican Club of Middletown, who met in 1888 when congressional candidate Charles H. Treat spoke. Treat would go on to some notoriety, not only becoming a Delaware congressman but also serving as twenty-first treasurer of the United States under both Theodore Roosevelt and William Howard Taft.

But perhaps most notable in the infancy of the Opera House, at least in the context of what the Opera House would later become, were those nights in its first thirty years when it showed pictures—not moving pictures, at least not yet, but pictures projected with light through lenses and onto a screen. In the early 1870s, the Opera House offered a collection of images, including scriptural views, landscapes, shots of Niagara Falls or public buildings in Washington, D.C., and even pictures of Venice, all for twenty-five cents and all projected via a Sciopticon, a version of a "magic lantern." As time passed, so too did image projection technology, and not long after the Sciopticon appeared at the Opera House, the Stereopticon showed pictures as well, at eighteen square feet (as advertised). When the Surricks brought their illustrated concerts to town in 1893, they used a Photo-Opticon to project "American and European wonders of art, architecture, statuary, etc."

FADE OUT

Come 1895, with nearly thirty years of success to the building's credit, new lessees George W. Ingram and Alex Maxwell renovated the entire town hall, readying the place for future screenings they had no idea were to come.

TAKE 2
THE NINETEENTH CENTURY

The (Opera) Housing Boom

FADE IN

It didn't take long for other cities and towns across the state to follow Middletown's suit. The last thirty years of the nineteenth century welcomed at least eighteen theatrical entities across the state's three counties. Two of those entities were located in parks. Eleven others were opera houses. Two of those opera houses are still open today.

OPENING CREDITS

Smyrna Opera House | 1870–circa 1923*
Como Theatre | 1931–1936
The Roxy | 1936–1948*
Smyrna Opera House | 2003–present
(Smyrna)

In 1869, a year after the ceremony at the Middletown Opera House, the Town of Smyrna committed to build for its citizens a town hall and did so in the winter of 1870. Like Middletown, Smyrna's Old Town Hall was a three-story brick structure serving multiple purposes. The first floor included a room for the town commissioner, a library and a jail. On the second floor was a meeting hall, and on the third floor was a Masonic Lodge. The Opera House itself wasn't called as such until 1886, when an extension was added to the building and a stage was added within the hall.

The Smyrna Opera House played host to myriad functions and events in its first thirty years, including locally cast plays, appearances by elocutionists and speakers, a performance by the Wilmington Minstrel Club, a cantata to benefit a local church and commencement exercises for Smyrna High School. The Opera House also hosted the Sixteenth Annual Colored State Teacher's Institute. One function of note was a reception in 1889 for Senator-elect Anthony Higgins hosted by the Duck Creek Hundred Republican Club. On the guest list that night were Charles H. Treat, who had spoken the previous year at Middletown, and, from Philadelphia, retail magnate John Wanamaker, himself on the verge of becoming the country's thirty-fifth postmaster general.

Dover Opera House | 1870–1900*
Dover Opera House/Nixon's Opera House/New Dover Opera House | 1904–circa 1930
Capital/Capitol Theatre | circa 1930–1982*
Schwartz Center for the Arts | 2001–2017
(Dover)

As mentioned previously, some theatrical entities start, stop and later begin anew. Also as mentioned previously, there are many different ways to carve up a theatrical population to produce firsts. The Dover Opera House fits both those bills. The more commonly known Dover Opera House was built in 1904 and would go on to a very long, albeit interrupted, history. But before *that* Dover Opera House, there was a previous Dover Opera House that opened in 1870. This circumstance gives the Dover Opera House the distinction of being the first known theatrical entity to have been built that would later close and reopen years later under the same name.

Sharing a building with the courthouse, the third-floor Dover Opera House (1870 edition) offered fare similar to that presented by the young opera houses located at points north. One such event occurred in September 1886, when James Barton, proprietor of the Wilmington burlesque house known as the Novelty Theatre, brought entertainment to the state capital. Two months later, though, Barton was found guilty in Wilmington of selling liquor without a license. While coincidental, this event preceded by several years some temperance meetings held at the Opera House, just as such meetings had been held in Middletown. Temperance was a recurring theme in the old days.

Late in the century, there was an appetite to build a new opera house. Funds were raised and a committee to manage those funds formed, but when the committee failed to appear in levy court to make its request official, the plan was considered abandoned.

Grand Opera House | 1871–1930
Grand Theatre | 1930–1967*
The Grand | 1969–present
(Wilmington)

While Middletown, Smyrna and Dover enjoyed their new opera houses, Wilmington was still without a proper theater. Coincidentally, Wilmington Masons were without a proper meeting hall. This led the Masons to form the Masonic Hall Company in 1869. To raise capital, the Masons sold stock in that company, and by the end of 1870, they had made enough to purchase the land between 814 and 822 Market Street. In January 1871, construction began.

The grand opening of the Grand Opera House took place on December 22, 1871, less than a year after groundbreaking. The building was huge, measuring 211 by 92 feet, with four stories of retail and Mason space to accompany the auditorium, itself 133 by 75 feet and 49 feet high (the third largest of its kind in the country). Opening festivities began at 9:00 p.m. with a musical program that ran until 11:00 p.m., after which people were invited to the floor to dance, which they did until 3:00 a.m.

The formal dedication took place on Christmas Day that year, which was followed by a week's worth of plays from the Wallack-Richings Dramatic Combination. Over its early years, the Grand Opera House served as Wilmington's entertainment destination; in addition to traveling troupes, the likes of Buffalo Bill Cody, John Philip Sousa and Lillie Langtry performed. It also provided a place for the community to host political events, lectures, commencements and so forth. The Wilmington Chorus made its debut on the Grand stage.

But the Grand Opera House also embraced the less traditional, and there are moments in its early history that pointed in the direction of moving

A postcard featuring the Grand Opera House, 818 North Market Street, Wilmington (1908). *Delaware Public Archives, Dover, Delaware.*

pictures. In 1877, Thomas Edison's Electromotograph made its appearance there. Music was played at Philadelphia's Western Union Telegraph Office and transmitted to the stage at the Opera House, in essence giving a concert by telephone. A lecture about how it worked accompanied the concert. Despite the technological display, the event was poorly attended.

As the century drew to a close, the Grand Opera House began its embrace of moving pictures. In October 1896, as part of a larger program, the Grand showed pictures via Lumière's Cinématographe. Other projection devices brought into the Grand for entertainment included an Animatagraph, Edison's Vitagraph, a Motograph, a Veriscope and Lubin's Cineograph.

The popularity of projected images was growing. The proprietors of the Grand Opera House seemed to sense that.

Historic Movie Theaters of Delaware

Milford Opera House | circa 1872–circa 1931
(Milford)

In Milford, the manager of the recently opened Milford Opera House came under fire from local media. As reported by the *News Journal* in 1872, the local Milford paper *News and Advertiser* "seems to delight in saying unjust and unkind things about Mr. Ford's management of the new Opera House." Ford's fate is unclear, but what appears to be a new opera house came along around 1881.

New Castle Opera House | 1879–circa 1954
(New Castle)

In 1879, the cornerstone for the New Castle Opera House, located on Delaware Street, was laid. The building, standing at fifty by one hundred feet, was similar to other opera houses of the time in that each of its three stories served specific purposes. The ground floor was used for business rooms, with the Opera House itself on the second floor. The third floor was used by both the Masons and the Odd Fellows.

In its early days, the New Castle Opera House was used as a rental hall and a roller skating rink, and it played host to numerous balls and other events. In 1890, New Castle High held its commencement exercises there. Celebrities Annie Oakley, Buffalo Bill Cody and Enrico Caruso all appeared there around the turn of the century.

The Auditorium | circa 1880–circa 1956
(Wilmington)

On what were previously circus grounds, the Auditorium, on West Eleventh Street, was built around 1880 in response to the roller skating craze that was overtaking the country; in fact, it was known as the Wilmington Roller Rink before incorporating. In 1894, it served as the site for the first-ever Wilmington Pure Food Exposition. Then, in January 1895, Professor Ernest Lacy conducted a "descriptive lecture" of *The Passion Play*, accompanied by illustrated moving pictures. The event was held nightly for a week, with matinees Wednesday through Saturday, for the admission price of twenty-five cents.

Armory Hall | circa 1884–circa 1946
Shore Theatre | 1946–circa 1955
(Milford)

I could find only one reference to Armory Hall prior to 1896. On April 11, 1884, a troupe called the Pauline Markham Combination played *Our Boys* in the hall. Moving ahead to 1896, what was referred to as a new hall was used for the first time in November to host the Sussex County Teachers' Institute. Through the remainder of the century, the hall played host to a variety of events, including dances and live shows.

Caskey Hall | 1885–1902
Newark Opera House | 1902–circa 1933
(Newark)

In 1885, Caskey Hall was built at 95 East Main Street. Previously in its place was a butcher shop and slaughter house that was a nuisance to the public. David Caskey bought the site, razed the structure and built his hall.

Brandywine Springs Park Theatre | 1886–1923
(Wilmington)

Prior to becoming the home of Brandywine Springs Amusement Park, New Castle County's first of two major seasonal attractions, there stood a hotel on Brandywine Springs Park, erected in 1826. The hotel became a private military school in 1853 but burned down that same year. After several changes of hand and an attempt at another hotel, Richard W. Crook eventually found success promoting the picnic grounds. Soon after, Crook added an amusement park. Access to the park was furnished by the Brandywine Springs Railway Company. Keeping with the tenor of the times, the park was temperate. It began showing motion pictures in 1899 in its Roof Garden Theatre.

Academy of Music | 1886–1888*
New Academy of Music | 1890–circa 1893
People's Theatre | 1893–circa 1894
The Bijou | 1895–1898
Academy of Music/New Academy of Music | 1899–1901
Wilmington Theatre | 1901–circa 1903
Lyceum | 1903–1908
Avenue | 1908–1912
Empire | 1912–1913
Avenue | 1913–1914
(Wilmington)

Located on a fifty-by-one-hundred-foot lot at 225 West Tenth Street, the Academy of Music would attempt to become the Grand Opera House's direct competition. Its January 11 open held promise, with a weeklong engagement featuring the Boston Ideal Opera Company and its fifty-six artists and fourteen-piece orchestra, all for a general admission price of fifty cents, or reserved seating for seventy-five cents or one dollar. But the theater's first season was plagued with financial troubles and lawsuits. Management was completely changed, but its financial troubles continued. Finally, in January 1887, business turned around under the third management group. Then, on the night of October 23, 1888, the Academy caught fire and burned to the ground. This appears to be the first fire of a theatrical entity that would eventually go on to show movies. It also appears to be the first time a theatrical entity had a break in its timeline and the first time one went through a name change, as the reopening of the theater—with the moniker the New Academy of Music—didn't occur until May 1890. Ownership changed hands in 1891.

August 1893 brought with it new ownership (again), new paint and fixtures and another new name, but the old troubles continued. By November, the renamed People's Theatre was sold (at sheriff's sale for the second time). It continued to operate under this name at least until February 1894. At some point between this date and August 1895, the theater went through another change and became the Bijou. That change didn't help the theater's fortunes either. In March 1897, the manager of the troupe performing there stopped the show mid-program and announced to the crowd that the theater had not paid the troupe; the show ended immediately. An incensed crowd stormed the box office to demand refunds, and the patrons physically removed the theater manager from the premises. Police needed to intervene.

In November 1898, the theater's electrician, due an unpaid salary, received a letter from the owners, who had gone to Washington for what was supposed to have been two weeks. The letter instructed the electrician to sell everything in the place, take what was owed to him and join them in Washington. With that, the Bijou simply closed. It reopened again in February 1899 and, perhaps hoping a return to its roots would bring a change of luck, took the name Academy of Music (sometimes referred to as the New Academy of Music). But the new name and the new century on the horizon wouldn't bring new luck to the old place.

Wilmington Musee | 1891–1892
Eden Museum/Wonderland Musee | 1892–1895
Wonderland (Music) Theatre | 1896–1903
Bijou Theatre | 1903–1904
(Wilmington)

When the Wilmington Musee opened at 309 Shipley Street, the *Evening Journal* described the exhibits the place would show as "living freaks," and the Musee didn't disappoint on its opening night when it featured Texas Jack Alexander, billed as a "Human Pincushion." There was also a mind reading act, as well as a comedy and musical company. Ten cents got visitors general admission; an extra nickel scored them reserved seats. The theater was later referred to in news items as the Eden Museum and the Wonderland Musee.

In 1895, owner William Dockstader moved his business to Seventh and Shipley Streets (his first relocation), and when the theater opened for the season in October 1896, it had an enlarged stage, a grand piano and a seating capacity of 1,400. Its new name was the Wonderland Theatre (a.k.a. Wonderland Music Theatre). Two months later, it would be the first theater in Wilmington, and in Delaware, to show what would become one of the most famous silent moving pictures in the history of film: William Heise's *The Kiss*. All eighteen seconds of the film, running at thirty frames per second, played on a Projectiscope.

Moving pictures continued to be part of Dockstader's regular roster, playing on projectors like the Cineographe, the Cinematographe and the Zimographe. In March 1898, the Wonderland Theatre met a fate similar to that of the original Academy of Music: a raging fire gutted the place. Not only was the theater destroyed, but the members of the company also lost most of their personal possessions. In June of that same year, Dockstader announced he would rebuild, and six months after the fire he did just that.

Shellpot Park Theatre | 1892–1934
(Wilmington)

At the foot of Penny Hill once stood Webster Mill. In 1892, that old mill property became the thirty-five-acre Shellpot Family Amusement Park, the second of Wilmington's two major seasonal venues to open in the late 1800s. Shellpot was the undertaking of the City Railway Company and was accessible by the Riverview electric line, which dropped off patrons at the park entrance. It began showing moving pictures around 1896–97.

Coulbourn's Opera House | circa 1897–circa 1926
(Seaford)

Coulbourn's Opera House, also referred to as the Seaford Opera House, has plenty of coverage but no concrete open or close dates. In fact, its first mention in November 1897 was in reference to the building being remodeled, followed by a masquerade party in December.

SEEKING STARDOM

At least four other opera houses and one theater opened or existed during the latter part of the nineteenth century, but in each of these cases, I was unable to ascertain if they had shown films in their history. Still, I want to include them here because they were places of entertainment, and since other similar places of entertainment in the era went on to show films, there is a good chance these places did too.

Odessa Town Hall/Odessa Opera House | 1876–1926
(Odessa)

In 1875, the *Middletown Transcript* reported that the town of Odessa was in need of a hall "wherein traveling performers could cater to their tastes." The Odessa Town Hall would open in 1876, and in its early years, the hall played host to various live performances similar to those at other halls and houses. The first specific reference to the Opera House I found was dated

1891, when an operetta and a farce were performed, with music by the Odessa Orchestra. I could find no connection between the hall and the house, but as other town halls and opera houses were often in the same building and often cross-referenced, I am including Odessa's two entities here as one. The most recent reference to the Opera House came in 1916 with a performance by the Delaware College Mandolin Club. The last reference to the town hall came in 1926, when it burned down.

Novelty Theatre | 1888–1889
(Wilmington)

James Barton, who had once brought entertainment to the Dover Opera House, opened his Wilmington burlesque house in 1888, only to leave it behind when he fled town with his wife in 1889. In that short time, the Bartons constantly ran afoul of the law, mostly on liquor charges, and their theater had a poor reputation.

Laurel Opera House | circa 1893–circa 1927
(Laurel)

A performance by the Laurel Amateur Comedians marks the earliest reference to the Laurel Opera House in February 1893. The house is also referred to in overlapping timelines (suggesting interchangeable names) as Bacon's Opera House and the New Opera House. In June 1899, a raging fire destroyed it, along with the Laurel business district and its eighty-four buildings. It was eventually rebuilt in 1900, and in 1909 it was the first hall in Sussex County to pay a license to the state. Its last mention found was in April 1927, when a musical was held to benefit the local fire company.

Harrington Opera House | 1896–circa 1900
(Harrington)

With local residents in need of an entertainment venue and the local militia in need of an armory, the Harrington Opera House came along in 1896 and served both purposes (offering the former a six-hundred-seat hall). What makes this opera house curious is how it relates to other theaters in

Harrington's history. E.C. Reese would build a new opera house around 1900 (often reported as 1903, but more on that later). His place would last until 1922 and be replaced by the Reese Theatre. The latest news appearance for any place referred to as the "Harrington Opera House" was 1922, the same year the Reese Opera House came to an end. I suspect the original Harrington Opera House closed when the Reese Opera House opened, and I suspect news reports, as they did with other opera houses around the state, casually referred to the Reese Opera House as the "Harrington Opera House" (read: the opera house located in Harrington).

Frederica Opera House | circa 1897–circa 1909
(Frederica)

I could find only three references to the Frederica Opera House in news accounts. The first was in reference to a cake walk that occurred in December 1897. The second was about a masquerade party that same month. The third was when the house was packed with four hundred people who came to hear Reverend A.W. Lightbourne preach in 1909.

FADE OUT

The turn of the twentieth century was a time of unbridled growth. Bigger houses were embracing film as part of their greater entertainment repertoire; smaller houses followed suit, as they were eager to offer their communities the same entertainment found in larger towns; and moviemakers, including producers, directors and projector inventors, were just getting started. Theaters were hot, film was heating up and the medium was on the verge of catching up to live entertainment as the primary entertainment choice for opera houses and the like. Eighteen theaters in a little over thirty years may sound like a lot, but the next thirty years would quadruple that number in new places.

TAKE 3
THE EARLY TWENTIETH CENTURY

Pictures, Moving

FADE IN

The first decade of the new century would find more than opera houses and town halls opening—it would also find theaters opening that would elevate films from minor additions to major presentations. During this decade, Wilmington would solidify itself as the theater capital of the state, adding eleven new entities to its geography (out of the twenty total statewide). It would lose a few theaters for the first time as well, including at least two that would open and close within the decade. Theaters would also find their way to the beach resorts of Sussex County.

OPENING CREDITS

Reese Opera House | circa 1900–1922
Reese Theatre | 1922–1943, 1945–1966
(Harrington)

Some sources cite the opening of the Reese Opera House as 1903, but news items report the Reese Opera House (or Reese's Opera House) was opened by E.C. Reese as early as 1900, with events being reported as having happened there between 1900 and 1903. In its first decade, the house hosted dances, graduations and meetings of the Farmers Institute.

Garrick Theatre | 1903–1930
(Wilmington)

William Dockstader, in his last years as proprietor of the Wonderland Theatre, had the buildings at 828–30 Market Street torn down, and in their spot he built the Garrick Theatre. Dockstader would be committed to live performances in his new 1,300-seat showplace, and in the spirit of opera houses, the giant hall was used for things other than vaudeville, like political events, YMCA meetings and Sunday services. Dockstader was also committed to newspapermen, as the Garrick was home to the city's first press box. Dockstader also knew the demand for moving pictures was great, and could he pick 'em. Just as he had shown *The Kiss* at his old place, at the Garrick, only a month after opening, Dockstader screened another future legend, Edwin S. Porter's *The Great Train Robbery*, on a Kinetograph. Film screenings would be a staple through the decade.

Garrick Theatre, 828–30 Market Street, Wilmington, 1906. *Delaware Public Archives, Dover, Delaware.*

Newark Theatre | 1904–circa 1958
(Newark)

In 1904, Newark citizens found themselves with a new entertainment option when the Newark Theatre opened its doors. In its opening's brief coverage, it was referred to as both an opera house and a playhouse.

Comedy Theatre | 1906–1907
Hyrup's Auditorium | 1907–1909
Red Moon Motion Picture Theatre | 1909–1913
Gem Theatre | 1913–1914
Comique Picture Palace | 1914–1915
(Wilmington)

In 1906, W.O. Hyrup was in the thick of Wilmington's first significant theater boom as he opened another of the state's firsts: Wilmington's first nickelodeon, the Comedy Theatre, at 402 Market Street. Admission was a nickel (thus the name) to see moving pictures and illustrated songs on a Cinematograph. By 1907, Hyrup had moved up the street to 411 Market, where he built a place to house a theater on the second floor and an arcade on the first. Hyrup's Auditorium opened to the public on March 23. In addition to moving pictures, Hyrup's showed prizefights and footage of the Wright brothers and their flying machine.

In 1909, the theater changed management and was renamed Red Moon Motion Picture Theatre. N.D. Cloward's intent was to create theme nights. Mondays and Tuesdays were dedicated to dramatic and historic subjects, travelogues were shown on Wednesdays and Thursdays and lighter fare screened on Fridays and Saturdays. One weekend late in the year, the Red Moon showed bullfighting from Spain.

The Bijou | 1906–1918
(Wilmington)

The Bijou, situated in an 18-by-117-foot building at 410 Market Street (across from the Comedy Theatre), was the third theater in Wilmington to bear that name.

11th Ward Theatre | 1906–1907
(Wilmington)

Throughout Delaware history, theaters of every type—opera houses, movie houses, drive-ins and multiplexes—have partnered with their communities. But no theater in Delaware's history had a connection with its community the way the 11th Ward Theatre did. Not only did it serve the community, but it also was literally built by the community. Located at Maryland Avenue and Beech Street, the three-thousand-seat open-air theater was built by the Citizen's Association of the Eleventh Ward, with proceeds to be used to pave the ward's streets.

That's right. The citizens of the ward built a theater to make money to pave their own streets.

The theater, sometimes referred to as the Unique Theatre, drew national attention, and on its opening night, a high-class vaudeville show was put on, including comedy, tragedy, musical numbers and a picture presentation on a Vitagraph. Minstrel shows, political events and other standard fare would follow, including popular amateur talent nights. Its first season ran from May to August 1906, and financially, it broke even. After adding a roof, the theater opened for a second season and offered more of the same types of entertainment, as well as life moving pictures and illustrated songs. It would be the theater's second and last season.

Moving Picture Place | 1906–circa 1907
Melodium | circa 1907
Nickelodeon | 1907–1908
Savoy | 1908–1950
Towne Theatre | 1950–1967, 1973–1975
(Wilmington)

On June 2, 1906, the Red Star Trading Stamp Company, located at 517 Market Street, went out of business. Shortly thereafter opened the Moving Picture Place, where for a nickel, pictures ran continuously all day and were changed twice weekly. In 1907, the theater was briefly called The Melodium, and it offered life moving pictures. Later that same year, ownership changed hands, and the theater changed its name to the Nickelodeon, but not even that name would last long for Wilmington's second five-cent theater. In 1908, it settled into the Savoy, and that's where it would stay for a very long time. One screening of note in its early existence came in 1909 when it was the first place in America (or so it advertised) to screen *The Great Earthquake of Italy*, which appears to have been a reference to the 1908 Messina earthquake.

Keller's Theatre | 1907–1941
(Bridgeville)

In 1907, Keller's Theatre was built. Also known as the Bridgeville Theatre, the six-hundred-seater was situated between the town's post office and fire hall.

Dreamland | 1907–circa 1908
(Wilmington)

Not content to own one theater on Market Street, W.O. Hyrup looked two blocks away from his Auditorium, toward 610 Market, where he opened Dreamland. It didn't get off to a very good start. While driving around town advertising the opening of the theater, the auto containing Hyrup and his two companions was struck by an electric car; Hyrup's car and advertising signs were ruined. Even though Dreamland opened that day, it wasn't long for existence. In January 1908, there was a small fire when a film ignited. No one was hurt and little damage was done, but that spurred members of several lodges that shared the building with Dreamland to file a formal complaint with the city council about the fire hazard the theater posed. The theater was sold later that year.

Connell Street Music Hall | 1908–1913
West End Theatre | 1914–1916
(Wilmington)

"The bride wore a white Duchess satin gown in princess style and carried pink and white carnations."

So read just one sentence from the *Evening Journal*'s account of the Statinko-Lutz wedding, which took place in January 1909 at the Connell Street Music Hall, 224 Connell Street. This was one such event hosted by the theater, which opened in the summer of 1908. The eight-hundred-seat venue offered vaudeville, dramas and moving pictures (sometimes with dancing after). It also billed itself as "the only theatre open in the city cooled by electric fans."

Pickwick Theatre | 1908–1921
(Wilmington)

Market Street continued its theater explosion when the Pickwick opened in the summer of 1908, also offering vaudeville and moving pictures, including films from the Cameraphone. One of the acts to appear at the theater was renowned escape artist Minerva. Despite her successful escape from a jump into the Christina River in police-inspected handcuffs, her appearance at the theater was interrupted when her manager was arrested for skipping out on a boarding bill. The constable took most of Minerva's effects, leaving her unable to perform.

Lewes Auditorium | 1908–1956*
Lewes Theater | 1964–1977
Lewes Cinema | 1977–1980
(Lewes)

On June 5, 1908, another cornerstone was laid in the state, this one in Sussex County for the Lewes Town Hall. Financed by the sale of stock, the town hall was not a building intended for government use (as was the case with most town halls around the state), but rather it was intended for use by the public as the public saw fit. Within that hall was the Lewes Auditorium where, in its beginning days, it played home to the traditional blend of vaudeville, local talent and moving pictures.

Lyric Theatre | 1908–1914
New Lyric | 1914–1916
Lyric | 1916–1919
Rialto Theatre | 1919–1979, 1981–1982
(Wilmington)

Market Street welcomed yet another theater in the first decade of the new century when the Lyric opened at 222 Market in October 1908. The Lyric, occupying the former Wilmington Candy Company building, offered vaudeville and life moving pictures for a nickel. Decades of tumult waited in its future.

Casino Moving Picture Theatre | circa 1909–1912*
Blue Hen Theatre | 1914–1956, 1959–1966
Beachwood Theatre | 1966–1980
(Rehoboth Beach)

The Casino Moving Picture Theatre (a.k.a. Casino Photoplay), likely Rehoboth's first theater, offered films on a seasonal basis that had been "passed by the National Board of Censorship in New York City."

Casino Moving Picture Theatre in Rehoboth, somewhere between 1909 and 1912. It appears the marquee was a chalkboard. *From the collection of the Rehoboth Beach Historical Society. Gift of Joan Hutchison.*

Palace Motion Picture Theatre | 1909–1911
The Star | 1911–1912, 1914
(Wilmington)

A block from the Lyric came Market Street, Wilmington and Delaware's last new theater of the decade, but it wasn't known for that. It was known for being the state's first theater that catered specifically to the black community. At 117 Market was the Palace Motion Picture Theatre, a four-hundred-seater that opened on October 9 to sellout crowds.

MOVING PICTURES

In addition to everything opening, it was a busy decade for the booming theater scene, and especially so for the Academy of Music. In 1900, when the City of Wilmington made it clear morality was the law of the land (a law that would rule the city and the state for decades to come), an actor appearing there was arrested for using "improper moral language" while in public. The words, which were not printed in the *Evening Journal*, were uttered as part of a performance, but this mattered not to police.

In 1901, the Academy changed its name (again) to the Wilmington Theatre, but problems would plague it in 1902, when a constable attached part of the theater's box office receipts to ensure four employees, who had not been paid, would be made whole. That attachment caused a shortage in the night's receipts, half of which were to go to the performing company. Because the performing company could not be paid, they refused to play.

Also in 1902, Newark's Caskey Hall was sold, another floor was added and it was renamed the Newark Opera House, with entertainment on the second floor of the brick building, a public hall and retail space on the first floor and more retail space on the third. As cited in its 1982 nomination for the National Register, the Opera House was "an important commercial and entertainment center for Newark residents at the turn of the century." It was the town's first nickelodeon and showed movies to both black and white patrons.

In 1907 Kent County, alcohol was on the mind of many. At the Dover Opera House, the "largest Sunday afternoon audience" convened to hear

The three-story building on the right is the original Middletown Town Hall; the Opera House is on the second floor, circa 1908. *Delaware Postcard Collection, University of Delaware Library, Newark, Delaware.*

Newark Opera House, 95 East Main Street (undated). *Delaware Public Archives, Dover, Delaware.*

Dickinson College president George Edward Reed give what was called a "stirring" temperance speech. But that was nothing compared to what happened at the Smyrna Opera House, when a well-known temperance play, *Ten Nights in a Barroom*, was scheduled to be performed. Those who ran the bars in town weren't thrilled with the idea of the show, so they worked together to get the bill changed at the last minute. The pro-temperance side, led by Smyrna Methodist Church pastor Robert Watt, cried censorship.

The Wilmington Theatre, which had changed its name in 1903 to the Lyceum, kept that name for about five years, but in 1908, its new shingle read Avenue Theatre. William Jennings Bryan spoke at the Dover Opera House, and the Grand announced its summer season would exclusively show moving pictures three times a day, changing films Mondays, Wednesdays and Fridays.

Fire safety was a serious issue in the 1900s. Early in the decade, managers of the Garrick and the Lyceum took extra precautions against the spread of fire, including installing extinguishers, firewalls, asbestos curtains and more. Later in the decade, inspections began at all sorts of businesses in the city, and in April, city council passed a new ordinance specific to motion picture theaters that addressed the issue of fire safety. The new rules mandated: projectors or their booths be enclosed in metal and lined with asbestos; smoking, as well as matches and lamp gas, be prohibited in the booth; and films be stored in fireproof containers.

Despite a 1903 showing of Georges Méliès's iconic *A Trip to the Moon* at Brandywine Springs, the film event of the decade may have taken place at the Lyceum in 1906, when the first recorded footage of the fires that raged in San Francisco in the aftermath of the earthquake was first screened in the country, two days ahead of any other city.

But the big story of the first decade of the new millennium took place at the Dover Opera House(s). In 1900, because the Opera House shared a building with the courthouse, the latter had an opportunity to save insurance money by closing the former, so the levy court did just that, leaving the citizens of Dover without a place of entertainment. Fundraising began immediately for the building of a new Opera House, and in 1904, at 226 South State Street, the second incarnation of the Dover Opera House opened its doors on May 9, with an address from Delaware Supreme Court justice James Pennewill and a presentation of the musical farce *Girls Will Be Girls*. In 1905, the Opera House abandoned farce for formality when it hosted Governor Preston Lea's inaugural ceremonies.

CLOSING CREDITS

In the 1900s, Delaware saw its first closure of one of the original nineteenth-century theaters.

1891–1904: Wilmington Musee | Eden Museum/Wonderland Musee | Wonderland (Music) Theatre | Bijou Theatre

What had begun as the Wilmington Musee in 1891 found not one short-lived existence in the new century, but two. William Dockstader, founder and sole owner of the entity at Seventh and Shipley, would go on to close the Wonderland Theatre in 1903 and open the Garrick. I would have considered keeping the Garrick as part of the Musee entity, since ownership remained the same and the closure of the Wonderland was directly connected to the open of the Garrick, but on Thanksgiving afternoon 1903, the Bijou opened where the Wonderland once stood. Its ad touted the theater as having formerly been Dockstader's, and its opening-day offering was the Turkish Bath Burlesquers. That was enough for me to keep the Garrick separate from this entity.

In January 1904, police shut down the performance of the Night Owls Burlesquers, deeming parts of the show immoral and vulgar, and threatening arrests if the show continued. Police also shut down the entire theater, citing the vulgar acts and the (remarkably coincidental) opinion the theater was not fire-safe. Since the theater's license was due to expire soon, police said they would speak to the clerk of the peace to see that it wasn't renewed. To the best of my knowledge, this was the first case of a Delaware theater being closed on morals charges.

SEEKING STARDOM

Delaware City Opera House | circa 1900–circa 1921
(Delaware City)

The Delaware City Opera House appeared in a national publication known as *Julius Cahn's Official Theatrical Guide* (volume 20, from 1921). It is listed in a section dedicated specifically to movie houses. In news items, a speech was reported to have been given there in 1900, and in 1908, the *Evening Journal* reported on a demonstration of a moving picture machine that promised otherwise high-priced operas for only ten cents.

Bridgeville Opera House | 1900–circa 1928
(Bridgeville)

Also in 1900, the Odd Fellows built a five-hundred-seat opera house (in addition to lodge accommodations and other rooms), where dances, commencement exercises and other events would be held at least until 1928.

Lewes Opera House | circa 1901–circa 1931
(Lewes)

The earliest reference to the Lewes Opera House I found was in 1901, when "an entertainment" was given by the Ladies' Guild of St. Paul's P.E. Church. There was also a suffrage event there in 1915, and in 1931, in keeping with Delaware's ongoing theme of temperance, a contentious meeting on the topic of prohibition took place—insults were hurled, and eventually, most of the five hundred attendees were dismissed.

Georgetown Opera House | circa 1902–circa 1932
(Georgetown)

The earliest and latest news items found on the Georgetown Opera House were both political events. In 1902, a Mississippi congressman addressed a Democratic meeting, while in 1932, a Maryland senator addressed Republican state candidates, including Governor Buck. During the three decades in between, traditional live entertainment and community events were conducted, and the building was one of fourteen affected by a massive fire in 1921.

Savoy Theatre | circa 1907 (Wilmington)

I struggled with where to include this. At first, I thought the references I found were connected to the Savoy on Market Street that had originally begun as the Moving Picture Place, but this Savoy was located at Third and King (and predated the other Savoy by at least a year). An ad in the *Evening Journal* promoted the theater's February 25 opening week of live acts and moving pictures. In March 1907, the theater was referred to as Herrmann's Savoy Theatre, and the final listing is found in the form of an ad on April 19.

FADE OUT

With most existing theaters from the 1800s still thriving, and with the burst of new theaters over the decade, the number of theaters open at a given time would peak at approximately thirty-three in 1909. There was much more to come.

LOST AND FOUND

Lost theater memories can be found around the state if you know where to look.

This original chair from the Lewes Auditorium is now part of the Lewes Historical Society archives. *Photo by Victoria Nazarewycz.*

TAKE 4
THE 1910s

The Rising South

FADE IN

Going into the 1910s, the overall growth of Delaware's theater scene was still bursting, but the majority of that boom happened south of Wilmington. Of the twenty-nine new theaters to appear during the decade, only eight debuted in the city, and of those eight, two would close during the same decade. Add to that another five older Wilmington theaters closing in the 1910s, and the state's theater hub would see a net growth of only one theater in ten years. Around the rest of the state, demand was strong and stable. All older theaters remained open for another ten years.

Boyd's Theatre | 1910–1916
(Dover)

What appears to be the first theater to open in the new decade would also be one of those theaters that would close within the same decade. Boyd's Theatre, housed in a former roller rink and touted as Dover's first movie house, was located on Loockerman Street between New and Queen. The building was constructed of galvanized iron, an important detail because in 1916, a fire started in the theater and its construction is credited with helping to prevent the fire from spreading to nearby buildings. That bit of good luck was offset by bad when a malfunction of fire alarms slowed firefighter response. The theater was a total loss. Uninsured owner William Boyd opted not to rebuild.

Hopkins Moving Picture Theatre | 1911–1914
Temple Theatre | 1914–circa 1915
Hopkins Theatre | circa 1915
(Wilmington)

Located at 1003 Orange Street, Hopkins was the second theater in the city to specifically cater to the black community. Throughout its brief history, it featured a blend of live acts and film features. In 1914, it changed its name to the Temple Theatre, and not long after that, even after advertising again as Hopkins, it closed.

Royal Motion Picture Theatre | 1911–circa 1916
(Rehoboth Beach)

The Royal Motion Picture Theatre, adjacent to a roller rink, first appears in news items in 1911, coexisting with the Casino. It is referenced in news items and photographs as both a motion picture theater and a home for vaudeville. The theater's last mention in news items was 1916.

Wright's Theatre/Wright's Auditorium | circa 1911–circa 1929
(Seaford)

One could say Jesse Wright was a Renaissance man. He got his start in the canning industry, which he followed with a shirt factory (a first for Seaford). In that shirt building, Wright opened Seaford's first motion picture theater and later expanded to the Auditorium on High Street. In addition to running pictures, Wright ran wiring to receive election returns and later had designs on digging a basement in his place so he could become an ice manufacturer. One summer, he limited screenings to Saturday nights because it was otherwise too hot, and another summer he converted the theater into an ice cream parlor because of a lack of interest in summertime movies. He allowed his place to be used for benefits, Red

Cross fundraising, Victory Liberty Loan meetings and even a murder inquest. But perhaps Wright's defining moment came in 1916.

In response to concerns over a smallpox outbreak, Seaford's board of health had, among other things, forbid people of color from attending movies. There was no such order issued for white people. Wright didn't think that was right, so he announced that anyone was welcome in his theater, regardless of race.

The Majestic Theatre | 1911–1927
(Wilmington)

The only theater to open on the 700 block of Market Street, located where St. Paul's Methodist Church once stood, was the Majestic, which boasted having a screen that was "scientifically and mathematically correct from every viewpoint." Although the theater's tenure was brief in comparison to other Market Street movie houses, its history was no less rich. In 1912, the theater found itself in the center of a moral controversy. The screening of films on Sundays was against the law. (These "blue laws" would carry on for decades.) A charitable Hebrew organization, the Woman's Bikur Chalim Society, had sold tickets to an exhibition of scriptural pictures at the theater. Complaints were filed with police, and the show was canceled.

But plenty of unique pictures did make it to the screen during the Majestic's first decade, like Kinemacolor Motion Pictures of the coronation of King George (the city's first screening of that event); a fifteen-minute reel of pictures from the *Titanic* disaster (one of the first screenings in the country); and the 1912 Indianapolis 500. Plus, the theater screened films covering local events, just one facet of its community involvement. Other facets included suffrage meetings, anti-saloon meetings, U.S. military recruiting aid, war drives and even one fundraiser that sent cigarettes to soldiers. The Majestic even offered something familiar to moviegoers of today: on-screen advertising (for the Wilmington Institute Free Library).

HISTORIC MOVIE THEATERS OF DELAWARE

Peoples Theatre | 1912–1920
Ryons Theatre | 1920–1931
Sussex Theatre | 1931–1941
Ayers Theatre | 1941–circa 1965
(Georgetown)

Peoples Theatre got off to a rocky start. No sooner was it built in 1912 than it was sold in 1913, but the theater manager had accepted another job in Philadelphia. Community usage was common in the decade.

Waller Theatre | 1913–1940
New Waller Theatre | 1941–1967
(Laurel)

In 1913, T.J. Waller built the Waller Theatre, and like other rural theaters at the time, it hosted various community events. As was the case in nearby Seaford, smallpox was a threat in Laurel, but here the theater shut down completely. In 1919, it played a six-reel picture, *The Price of Peace*, as part of a Victory Loan rally. The government-produced film, which depicts scenes of the war from the front lines, played to an estimated one thousand people (despite a seating capacity of eight hundred).

Showing ads before the main entertainment is nothing new. While probably not as annoying as some commercials that precede movies in theaters today, the ads onstage at the Waller Theatre (circa 1913) were no less intrusive. *Delaware Public Archives, Dover, Delaware.*

The Playhouse | 1913–1926
Schubert Playhouse | 1926–circa 1930
The Playhouse | circa 1930–2003
DuPont Theatre | 2003–2015
Playhouse on Rodney Square | 2015–present
(Wilmington)

On January 15, 1913, Wilmington's Hotel du Pont celebrated its grand opening. Three months later, construction began on another piece of the greater DuPont Building: The Playhouse. The 1,200-plus-seat theater was completed in 150 working days and boasted a fireproof stage that was larger than all but three stages in New York City. The opening-year schedule consisted of seventy-seven productions, eleven of which were motion pictures. The first motion picture played one month after the theater opened, via Webb Talking Pictures, displayed by a device called the Magnaphone, an invention of Wilmington native George R. Webb. Webb's films included *Faust* and *Casey at the Bat*.

Palace Theatre/Nixon's Palace Theatre | 1913–circa 1924
(Milford)

In January 1914, one month after the Palace Theatre opened on North Walnut Street, the theater played host to children from Avenue Methodist Episcopal Sunday School. This would begin the routine occurrence of the theater hosting events for the young people of Milford, including Christmas and Boy Scouts screenings in what has been identified as Milford's first silent theater. In 1918, a storm flooded the Mispillion River, which in turn flooded many merchants, including the theater, which would persevere.

Rex Theatre | 1914–1917
(Wilmington)

In addition to showing motion pictures, the Rex, at 738 Lincoln Street, hosted women's basketball for charity, as well as live entertainment provided by the Boy Scouts and the children of the local Neighborhood House.

Victoria Theatre | 1914–1920
(Wilmington)

While its tenure may have been relatively brief in the crowd of Wilmington theaters, the one-thousand-seat Victoria, at 836 Market, had a packed history, especially during its first year. The theater presented films in Kinemacolor and, on opening night, distributed programs listing the films that would be shown over the coming weeks. This was described by the *News Journal* as an "innovation" and would become something many theaters around the state would regularly do. The films shown at the Victoria were accompanied by an all-female orchestra.

A highlight of the theater's history included commissioning filmmakers to film troops breaking camp at the state rifle range before being transferred to New Mexico (and having the film prepared to screen the next night), as well as commissioning another film of those same boys returning to Delaware. And mindful of the morality of the times, the theater extended offers to local clergy to screen films for free and pull them if objectionable.

The Polonia | 1915–1922
Avenue Theatre | 1923–1936
Ace Theatre | 1936–1963
Capri Art Theater | 1963–1970
(Wilmington)

On March 20, 1915, in Wilmington's Polish section, at 405–7 Maryland Avenue, the 350-seat Polonia opened for its community. On its regular docket were Polish-language films and Catholic/religious pictures. Because it catered to such a specific audience, the theater didn't advertise much.

Elcora Theatre | 1915–circa 1934
Delmar Theatre | 1935–1944*
Avenue Theatre | 1946–circa 1954
(Delmar)

Tucked away in the southwest corner of the First State is Delmar, a town shared with the State of Maryland and dubbed "The Little Town Too Big for One State." On November 3, 1915, the Elcora, named for Cora

Ellis (wife of owner Seth Ellis), opened. The steam-heated, 450-seat brick theater started with a vaudeville act, and a confectioner with a soda fountain in his shop occupied the front of the building. In its early days, it played host to a political rally, a live community production and at least one Tom Thumb wedding.

The Theater at Fort DuPont | 1916–1945
(Delaware City)

Fort DuPont was one of four Delaware military bases to offer moving pictures to those stationed there. In 1916, no specific building existed to show pictures; instead, screenings occurred in the service hut and would continue to be shown there for close to twenty years. It was also the only movie theater in the state where movies were shown on Sundays (seemingly exempt from Delaware's blue laws). Civilians could take advantage of this because the public was allowed on base.

Queen Theatre | 1916–1959*
The Queen/The Queen Wilmington | 2011-Present
(Wilmington)

In a building at Fifth and Market that spent its first 127 years as a hotel (first the Indian Queen and then later the Clayton House), the Wilmington Amusement Company opened a two-thousand-seat movie palace called the Queen, and after receiving raves about everything from its architecture to its opening slate (the five-reeler *Between Men*, the Keystone comedy *Dizzy Heights and Daring Hearts* and a Universal newsreel), it kept its ongoing vaudeville, film programming and special events as relentlessly good throughout the 1910s.

The Queen also was a key component in the community, playing host to meetings for myriad groups: Irish, Republicans, shipbuilders, patriots and dry law supporters. Other events it facilitated included a benefit dance for firemen, a fundraiser for the Red Cross, Jewish war relief, the Salvation Army's twenty-fifth anniversary and a recruiting party for the military. Special screenings included *On the Firing Line with the Germans*, a film shot on the field of war by former Delawarean William H. Durborough; W.H. Farley's illustrated lecture *Wake Up America*, about the horrors of German warfare; private films for DuPont employees about things like social diseases and the company's guncotton plant; and a Kinogram that played a film depicting the implosion of a local building.

Its roster of in-person guests may have eclipsed all of that. Silent film stars Rose Tapley and J. Warren Kerrigan made appearances (on separate occasions); William Jennings Bryan spoke about the benefits of prohibition for the Anti-Saloon League; Anne Morgan, daughter of the late J.P. Morgan, spoke on the devastation of France and screened *The Heritage of France*; and in 1918, former U.S. president William Howard Taft spoke at a political rally.

National Theatre | 1916–1951
Hopkins Theatre | 1951–1958
(Wilmington)

Although it was open to all, the National Theatre at 810–12 French Street was the third theater in the city to specifically cater to the black community. It was built by Dr. Samuel G. Elbert, one of Delaware's first licensed black physicians. The National offered everything the other city theaters did: free movies for kids, church services on Sundays, political events, benefit screenings, a dry rally, live wrestling and even a screening of a government-made film about the perils of venereal disease called *Fit to Fight*.

But the National was also an important location for the African American community to convene. In its first few years, it was the site of numerous meetings about education, race riots in Washington, D.C., and the memorialization of black servicemen lost in World War I. It also screened the first and only five-reel picture produced by people of color: *The Colored American Winning His Suit*. The film was produced by the Frederick Douglass Film Company.

Temple Theatre | 1917–circa 1956
(Dover)

With Boyd's Theatre having burned down in 1916, the state capital was again home to only one entertainment venue, the Dover Opera House. Enter the summer of '17 and the opening of the 425-seat Temple Theatre in the Odd Fellows Temple on Loockerman Street. The opening of the theater also marked the debut of future Delaware theater magnate George M. Schwartz. In its early years, several screenings were partnered with

Over a dozen men (and a horse) stopped the groundbreaking of Dover's Temple Theatre to pose for this photo, circa 1917. *Delaware Public Archives, Dover, Delaware.*

government organizations, including a war picture during a 1917 patriotic rally, a six-reel presentation as part of a Victory Loan event in 1919 and a lecture on public health coupled with a health film.

Dodd's Hall | circa 1919–circa 1930
(Millsboro)

While concrete open/close dates are scarce, Dodd's Hall (sometimes called Dodd's Theatre) first appeared in the news in 1919 when it played host to a school meeting. It also played silent films.

Fox Theatre | 1919–circa 1930
Milton Theatre | circa 1930–1969, 2003-2010, 2014-Present
(Milton)

The citizens of Milton wanted a theater, so Ida Fox modified a room above her Union Street store to be used for just such a thing, creating the five-hundred-seat Fox Theatre. Ida's son, William H. Fox, would run the business until his untimely passing in September of that same year. Ida took over the theater and, in doing so, became one of the first female theater managers in the state's history.

Royal Theatre | 1919–1928
Elaine Theatre | 1928–1930
Colonial Theatre | 1930–circa 1933
Earle Theatre | 1933–1977
(New Castle)

The opening of the Royal Theatre in New Castle is a bit of a mystery. There is a one-sentence announcement in the September 16, 1919 *Morning News* saying the "new motion picture theatre at Fifth and Delaware Streets held its opening [the night before]." However, an ad in the *Evening Journal* announced the "Grand Opening of The Royal Theatre" on February 7, 1920. I've always considered daily newspapers to be real-time diaries of events of the past, and while they certainly aren't infallible, in this instance, and in the absence of further evidence, I'll presume the 1919 open date was what's known today as a "soft open," with the formal open happening in 1920.

MOVING PICTURES

Screening technology continued to evolve around the state in the decade. At the Grand, the Harrisograph and the Grandograph were used to show moving pictures early in 1910. The Savoy was projecting on the "Wonder Screen," which management touted as allowing them to show pictures, without negative effect, while the theater was brightly lit. And while movies may have been gaining in popularity, there was still news to be made on the stage, including the appearance of acting royalty Lionel Barrymore at the Garrick.

Fire safety continued to be an important issue in Wilmington early in the decade. The public building committee filed a report with the city council, citing fire concerns with specific theaters, including the Pickwick for having no rear exits, the Avenue for having insufficient exits and the

HISTORIC MOVIE THEATERS OF DELAWARE

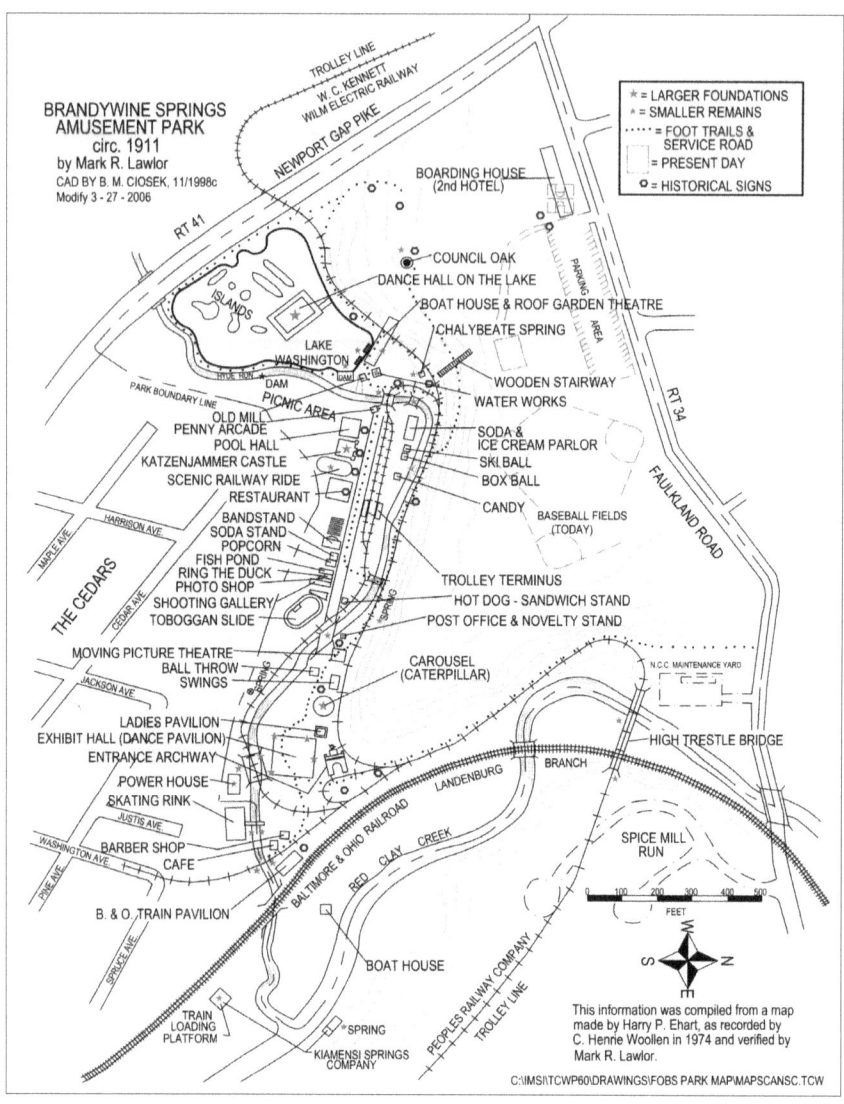

Brandywine Springs Park as it looked circa 1911. The theater is located slightly below and to the left of center, between the toboggan slide and the ball throw. *From the personal collection of Mark L. Lawlor.*

Garrick and Grand for failing to house their projectors in booths. Also in the report was the concern that theater aisles were not being kept as clear as they should have been. This led to a new ordinance prohibiting theater overcrowding.

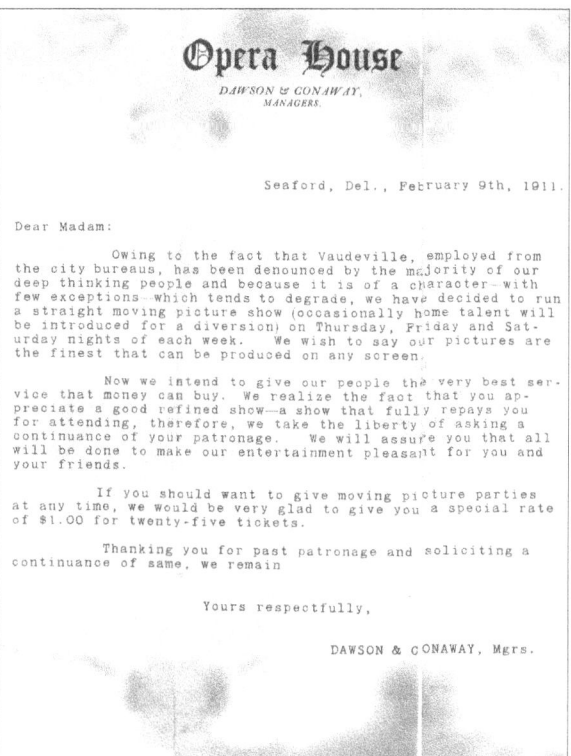

This letter, which reads as if it is in response to a complaint, is from the managers of Coulbourn's Opera House in Seaford. Not only does this confirm the Opera House showed pictures, but it's also a great early example of how the morality of the community drove theaters to take decisive action. *From the personal collection of Sue Bramhall.*

Social struggles dominated 1913. A shooting incident at Coulbourn's Opera House led Seaford Town Council to ban entertainment for people of color in 1914. The Garrick and the Avenue also banned people of color.

In 1915, unique moments were happening. A delegation of prominent Wilmington women petitioned the city to allow movies to be shown on one particular Sunday in April to raise money for war relief. Theaters were on board (of course), and the council did not oppose the project. That same year, a motion picture was introduced as evidence for the first time in U.S. District Court history, and those involved in the patent case went to the Victoria to watch the film. Also that year, the World Series between the Philadelphia Phillies and the Boston Red Sox was put on display at the Dover Opera House. Lights were arranged onstage to simulate a baseball diamond, and as plays were wired to the theater, the lights would change accordingly.

In 1916, the smallpox epidemic that gripped the state forced the temporary closure of many businesses, including the Playhouse; staying north, Brandywine Springs Park was sold and the theater stopped

On one side of this original program from the Smyrna Opera House is the list of every film slated to screen in October 1919. On the opposite side, a picture of silent film star Dorothy Gish, whose films *Nugget Nell* and *Nobody Home* were on the slate. *Courtesy of the Smyrna Opera House.*

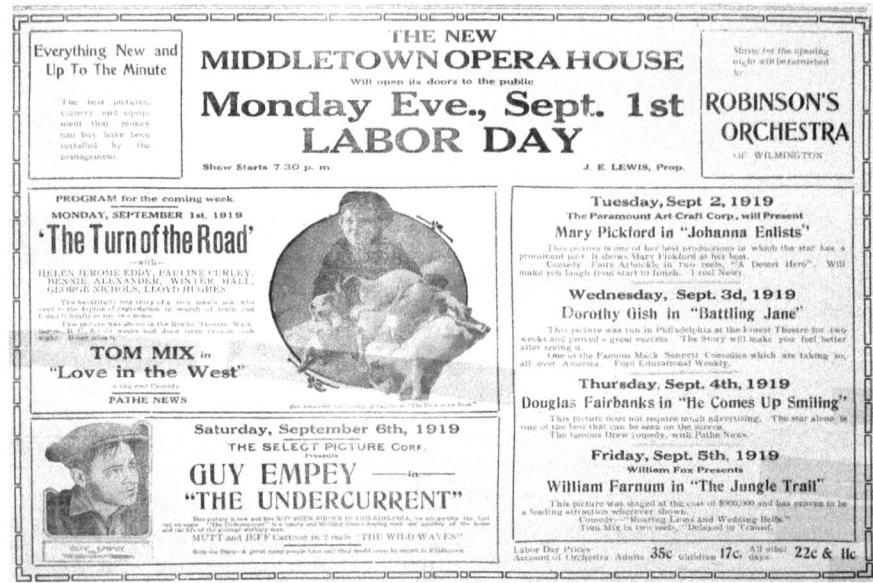

When the Middletown Opera House was rebuilt after its first fire, it reopened with a slate of films starring luminaries of the era, including Mary Pickford and Douglas Fairbanks, two of the founders of United Artists (via the *Middletown Transcript*). *Middletown Historical Society.*

showing films. In 1917, a new war tax went into effect on amusements. In government-related theater activity in 1918, the Dover and Newark Opera Houses held Liberty Loan drives, the Smyrna Opera House hosted the committee on patriotic addresses and the Savoy sold bonds. Later in the decade, the Lyric settled into its new name: the Rialto.

Fire safety may have been the focus in Wilmington in the 1910s, but fire losses were an even bigger story south. In 1912, Rehoboth's Casino Moving Picture Theatre would fall to a devastating blaze. In the early-morning hours of August 17, a fire broke out between Rehoboth and Baltimore Avenues. The theater was destroyed, as were the adjacent auditorium and roller rink; five other stores were lost. While it was the end of the Casino, it wasn't the end of movies in Rehoboth, or even the end of movies where the Casino had stood. In 1914, the Blue Hen Theatre was built to replace it.

A bigger story still—perhaps the biggest of the 1910s—unfolded on New Year's Eve 1918, when the Middletown Opera House, home of the first opera house and the oldest Masonic lodge in Delaware, burned to the ground. The afternoon blaze of unknown origin spread quickly, thwarting the efforts of fire companies from Middletown, Smyrna, Port Penn, Delaware City and Wilmington. Two adjacent buildings, one of which was the post office, also suffered significantly.

Middletown was undaunted. A new Opera House was built in the same spot as the original, and it reopened on Labor Day 1919. The opening slate consisted of a Pathé newsreel, the two-reel Tom Mix comedy *Love in the West* and the main feature, the King Vidor drama *The Turn in the Road*.

CLOSING CREDITS

1886–1914: Academy of Music | New Academy of Music | People's Theatre | The Bijou | Academy of Music/New Academy of Music | Wilmington Theatre | Lyceum | Avenue | Empire | Avenue

After starting as the Academy of Music in 1886 and spending more than twenty years being plagued with money and identity problems, what came into the new decade as the Avenue Theatre was seized by the sheriff and sold yet again in 1911. The next year, the theater changed its name to the Empire Theatre, but its money woes remained the same. After its last name change (back) to the Avenue, the theater finally met its ultimate fate. During a screening of *Rose of the Ranch*, a blaze broke out, and the building was a complete loss. About $75,000 in damage was estimated to have been done, with insurance covering only $30,000 of that. For one last time, the theater was short on cash.

1909–1914: Palace Motion Picture Theatre | The Star

In 1911, the Palace changed its name to the Star and found itself under new management. Neither of these events was uncommon. What was uncommon was that in two short years, the city's first theater to serve the black community would be converted to whites-only. In February 1911, the *Evening Journal* reported the theater would close for renovations and when it reopened it would be "for white patronage exclusively." It went through a second remodel then closed in 1912. After repairs, it reopened briefly in 1914 but closed that same year.

1906–1915: Comedy Theatre | Hyrup's Auditorium | Red Moon Motion Picture Theatre | Gem Theatre | Comique Picture Palace

The early 1910s brought more bad luck to another Market Street theater when legal troubles hounded Red Moon, including improper licensing, an issue with showing prizefight images and that time a theater employee assaulted a fifteen-year-old. The theater was sold and renamed the Gem Theatre in 1913. It would go through one more name change to the Comique Picture Palace in 1914, then close under that name in 1915.

1908–1916: Connell Street Music Hall | West End Theatre

In 1910, the Connell Street Music Hall, occasionally referred to as Kruger's Hall, was at the center of a near-scandal. It was rumored that on a given evening, a dinner was being held for men only, and at this men's dinner there would be three female dancers "of the 'Salome' kind" (per the *Evening Journal*). Undercover police were ready to arrest, but nothing happened. The theater would go on to close in 1913, reopen in 1914 as the West End Theatre, then close again for good in 1916.

1906–1918: The Bijou

Perhaps lost in the flurry of Market Street theaters, the Bijou lasted a little more than a decade. In 1918, the building was sold to the owners of the restaurant next door in what was reported as one of the largest real estate deals of the time. The restaurateurs had designs of expanding their place into the theater property.

SEEKING STARDOM

Nine additional theaters established some kind of presence in the 1910s, many of which were on record as having shown films. Again (and still sadly), there wasn't enough supporting evidence to include them in the main timeline.

Delmar Opera House | circa 1910–circa 1923
(Delmar)

The first news mention I found of the Delmar Opera House appeared in a 1910 edition of the *Philadelphia Inquirer*. The local high school was putting on a play at the theater. A smattering of other mentions includes political meetings and commencement exercises, and in 1923, county agricultural films played there.

Greenwood Opera House | circa 1911–circa 1933
(Greenwood)

This theater is possibly also known as Houseman's Auditorium, the Greenwood Auditorium and/or the Greenwood Theatre. Mentions of these names are fluid over time, but no two names ever appear at the same time to suggest they were different places. While I'm confident they are all the same place, I could find no direct connection among them. Silent movies were shown "here" in 1912.

Star Theatre | circa 1912
(Newark)

This is the second of three Star Theatres in Delaware in the 1910s, but there are few records. According to the *Newark Post*, charity screenings for the Newark Library and other community causes were routine here. The first appearance I found was in April 1912, and the last was December that same year, when it moved from a location across from Powell's Restaurant to Centre Hall on Main Street.

Bruner's Hall | circa 1912–circa 1918
(Delaware City)

I first found Bruner's in the *Julius* guide, and further research turned up nothing concrete in terms of open or close dates. The theater did show films, at least from 1914 forward, and hosted public events.

Lyceum Theatre | circa 1913
(Lewes)

According to the *News Journal*, John M. Vessels leased the Lyceum Theatre to W.C. McDaniels, who "inaugurated a new series of motion pictures." Further information remains elusive.

Star Theatre | circa 1915–circa 1918
(New Castle)

The third theater to bear the Star name in the same decade participated in Liberty Loan campaigns, and there is a mention of a 1915 presentation of something called *St. Elmo*, which could have been the 1914 film. The theater shared an alley with Ahearn's Barber Shop, on or near Delaware Street.

Temple Theatre | circa 1918–circa 1919
(New Castle)

Common, too, was the name Temple for Delaware theaters, but the one in New Castle at 410 Delaware Street didn't have much to reveal. It showed films, including a Mary Pickford seven-reeler and the western serial *The Terror of the Range*, which ran seven weeks. Given the earliest appearance I found was 1918, and given New Castle's Star Theatre seems to close in 1918, it is possible the places are the same, but I found nothing to link them.

Ellendale Motion Picture Theatre | 1919–circa 1921
(Ellendale)

The Ellendale, a.k.a. Tropical Theatre, was another *Julius* find. In the years there were news mentions, films are confirmed to have played there (some for charity), and the theater was used by a local church for Sunday services.

Virginian Theatre | circa 1919
(Middletown)

With only the Opera House as an entertainment venue in Middletown, the Virginian opened in May 1919 and showed a variety of films, from Tom Mix to Mutt and Jeff, as well as World's Kinograms, but a management change four months into the theater's life may have suggested other issues. October 1919 is the last record I found for the theater, but a 1920 news item mentions the Middletown Hotel, "where the Virginian Movie Theatre was," confirming the theater's short life.

FADE OUT

The 1910s were the decade of Delaware's greatest theatrical growth (a statistic that still holds today). But even with a peak number of forty-eight open theaters in 1916 and 1919, the state still had yet to hit its single-year maximum number of open venues.

LOST AND FOUND

Lost theater memories can be found around the state if you know where to look.

This original cash drawer (*top*) from the Waller Theatre is now part of the Laurel Historical Society archives. *Photo by Victoria Nazarewycz.*

This original Newark Opera House stock certificate from 1914 (*bottom*) is available to view at the Newark Historical Society. *Courtesy of the Newark Historical Society.*

TAKE 5
THE 1920s

Volume

FADE IN

In terms of open theaters per specific decade, Delaware's maximum build-count peaked in the 1910s, but that wave of growth actually carried through 1921, the year in Delaware's history it had the most open theaters in one calendar year: fifty-nine. And on the horizon for the forty-six (of those fifty-nine) theaters that made it to 1929?

Nothing much. Just sound.

OPENING CREDITS

Frankford Opera House | 1920–1930
(Frankford)

In 1919, Benjamin M. Jones built a stable at the corner of Knox and Reed Streets. A year later, he converted the structure to a theater and called it the Frankford Opera House, but it wasn't as easy as it sounds. In 1920, the town had no electricity, so Jones used an eight-horsepower gas engine to generate power to run his single Simplex projector. (A second projector was eventually added.) Tickets were twelve cents, and pictures shown there included Hoot Gibson westerns and D.W. Griffith's *The Birth of a Nation*. Meetings and school plays were conducted there, as were programs from traveling troupes. Jones also projected ads from local merchants on his screen.

Green Lantern Theatre | 1920–circa 1939
Don Theatre | 1940–1941
Pike Theatre | 1941–circa 1952
(Claymont)

At the northeast end of the state, at the corner of Philadelphia Pike and Myrtle Avenue, opened Claymont's Green Lantern Theatre. On opening night, the theater showed the Cecil B. DeMille adventure *Male and Female*. Along with screenings and the usual community needs, the Green Lantern played host to the first-ever meeting of the Delaware Building and Loan Association.

The Strand | 1920–1952
(Wilmington)

One of five theaters to come to life in the state in 1920, the Strand opened on May 14 at 2412 Market Street with a screening of *Leave It to Me*. The theater's music was furnished by a full string orchestra, and the lighting changed color with each picture shown.

Victory Theatre | 1920–1923
Hunt's Theatre | 1923–1924
Broadway Theatre | 1924–1930
(Wilmington)

Adorned in the flags of the Allied forces, the Victory Theatre opened in June 1920 at 1715 West Fourth Street. In its first year, in addition to vaudeville and film, the theater was active in the Italian community, including playing host to meetings for the Italian Earthquake Relief Committee. But the theater's big get in its first year was former congressman and future New York mayor Fiorello La Guardia, who was the principal speaker at a meeting of Italian

Republicans. Theater ownership would change several times, as would its name, to Hunt's Theatre in 1923 and the Broadway Theatre in 1924.

Park Theatre | 1920–1952, 1954–1967
(Wilmington)

The 1,100-seat Park Theatre was located at 307 Union Street and hosted a pair of peculiar local screenings in the 1920s. One, in 1925, showed a collection of old buildings around the state, all slated for preservation. The other, from 1923, showed views of the powder mills along the Brandywine as they existed when they were in operation. This was believed to have been the only motion picture in existence to depict the oldest powder manufacturing plant in the world. At the end of the decade, the theater installed a Western Electric Reproducing System to accommodate true talking pictures.

The Arcadia | 1921–1956
(Wilmington)

The Arcadia, at 510 Market Street, got off to something of an odd start. Where most theaters go through name changes during their lifetimes, the Arcadia went through one before it opened. Originally conceived as the Princess Theatre, the public was instead asked to vote on what the theater's name should be; options included Colonial, Bluebird, Apollo and Ideal. The winning entry was the Wilart, but the owners didn't think the name was appropriate, so instead they went with Arcadia (from another entrant). Waivers were requested from entrants whose ideas received more votes than Arcadia, and the theater received "favorable replies in the majority of the cases." The opening film was *The Nut*, starring Douglas Fairbanks.

The theater held numerous contests throughout the 1920s, and the best may have been won by local affianced couple Elsie Kafader and George Roberts. They won a contest that showered them with gifts from local merchants, including furniture, china, clothing, price reductions on a car and a house, baby items and cash. The couple was then married *in the theater*, with a full audience to bear witness. It was all in conjunction with the screening of the film *Deserted at the Altar*. Really. (Postscript: The couple was still married at the time of George Roberts's death on Christmas Day 1946.)

In 1925, Warner Bros. bought the Arcadia, which paved the way for the theater to install Vitaphone, a Warner-owned system, in 1928. This made the Arcadia the exclusive Vitaphone house in Wilmington, so when true sound screenings began with Warner Bros.' *The Jazz Singer*, the Arcadia was the place to go, as evidenced by the nearly three thousand people who attended the first day. Later that year, the Arcadia installed Movietone.

Liberty Theatre | 1921–1922
(Wilmington)

Disappearing almost as quickly as it appeared was the Liberty, located at Heald and Apple Streets on the city's east side. Like the National and the Hopkins Moving Picture Theatre before it, the Liberty catered specifically to the black community—only it didn't last nearly as long as those others. Despite providing moving pictures and live entertainment, the theater closed in 1922 and became a rescue mission.

Palace Theatre | circa 1921–circa 1923
Strand Theatre | 1923–circa 1945*
Smyrna Theatre | 1948–circa 1973, circa 1979–circa 1981
(Smyrna)

For fifty years, the Opera House was Smyrna's only source of theatrical entertainment. That changed in 1921 when, at the corner of Delaware and Commerce Streets, Horace David built the Palace Theatre. But it wasn't long before the theater was sold to Mark McManus, who used to show films in the Smyrna Town Hall. With that 1923 sale came a name change to the Strand. The first film shown was *Robin Hood* (most likely the 1922 version starring Douglas Fairbanks). In 1927, the theater changed hands again. It kept its now-familiar name, and the buyer was familiar, too: George Schwartz, owner of the Temple Theatre in Dover (and manager of the Opera House there as well). Renovations were made in 1928 to accommodate vaudeville.

The Aldine | 1921–1941
Loew's Aldine | 1941–1970
(Wilmington)

Muscling-in not only on a crowded Market Street but also on a crowded 800 block of Market Street (where the Grand and the Garrick were already established) was the Aldine, and to make an opening statement, the first film it screened was D.W. Griffith's *Dream Street*, with two of the film's stars, Ralph Graves and Charles Emmett Mack, appearing in person to promote the film. By 1922, ownership had changed hands, and the new owners wanted to use the theater for more traditional vaudeville entertainment, which included a local talent contest where winners would receive a contract to play live at the theater. In 1925, the theater was purchased by Warner Bros. and remodeled.

Parkway Theatre | 1921–1922*
Adams' Parkway Theatre | 1924–circa 1925*
Parkway Theatre | 1928–circa 1931
Loew's Theatre | 1931–1941
Ritz Theatre | 1941–1962
(Wilmington)

Located at Delaware Avenue and Adams Street and billed as "The Down Town Theatre in Walking Distance," the Parkway opened with 1,200 seats on July 30. It was the exclusive theater of First National Exhibitors, and it would screen films that had not played in Wilmington before. The opening slate featured Kineto Reviews (short films of varied subjects ranging from nature to travel and the human condition), the comedy *The Toonerville Trolley that Meets All Trains* and the drama *Man, Woman, Marriage.*

That promising open was short-lived. In February of the following year, the independent theater unexpectedly closed, mostly due to rapidly declining patronage and the heavy expense of securing films. After closing, it was occasionally used for special screening events. One notable screening was in early 1924, when the press was invited by William G. Taylor, former Wilmington mayor, to an exhibition of the Phonofilm, an audio/visual synchronization device that was the precursor to the Vitaphone. (Taylor was president of Phonofilm Finance Inc.) This screening would later be cited as the first sound screening, albeit a private one, in the city.

In December 1924, the theater formally reopened as the Adams' Parkway Theatre, under new ownership and management, but the restart hit an early snag. It had intended to screen *The Birth of a Nation*, but it was warned if it did, people would be arrested. The city invoked an ordinance passed in 1915 to prevent "bad feelings" between the black and white communities. The theater closed again for unknown reasons in 1925, only to return to life in 1928 (back to just the Parkway Theatre). New York investors remodeled the place, installed a Photophone and screened DeMille's *The King of Kings* for its grand reopening. Then, in 1929, it found amazing success hosting a series of lectures on cooking, a niche that would propel it into the next decade.

New Theatre | 1921–1933
Palace Theatre | 1933–circa 1961
(Seaford)

W. Ford Breeding, manager of the Opera House in Federalsburg, Maryland, opened the New Theatre in Seaford at the corner of High and Market Streets, opposite the Hotel Sussex. The theater was equipped with a stage for non-film needs, including minstrel shows, community events and, in 1923, a pro-KKK rally. For its five-year anniversary, the theater went through a cosmetic upgrade, as well as an upgrade to its twin projectors, and in 1929, Breeding installed the equipment necessary to show talking pictures.

Plaza Theatre | 1922–1927
New Plaza Theatre | 1928–1939
Schine's New Plaza Theatre | 1939–1946
Community Plaza Theatre | 1946–1948
Milford Theatre/Schine's New Milford Theatre | 1948–1972
(Milford)

In 1922, J.E. Lewis of Middletown built in Milford the Plaza Theatre, a brick, steel, concrete and tile building, with seven hundred seats on the floor and another five hundred in the balcony, to be used for motion pictures every evening, "clean vaudeville" twice a week, plus plays and public uses. At the time, it was the largest theater south of Wilmington. Its opening-night feature, after a series of speeches, was *Why Girls Leave Home*. In addition to entertainment and wildly varied community use (everything from a KKK meeting to the Prettiest Girl in Milford contest), the first few years also included a pair of special visitors to the theater.

In November 1922, on behalf of the Republican ticket, Assistant Secretary of the Navy (and presidential son) Theodore Roosevelt Jr. spoke. And in June 1923, President Warren G. Harding, along with the First Lady and an entourage of others, paid a visit to Delaware that began in Wilmington but had a lengthy stop in Milford where, at the Plaza, the president was initiated into the Order of the Tall Cedars of Lebanon (a side degree of Freemasonry).

The good times of the decade didn't last long, though. The theater went into foreclosure and was eventually sold in 1927. After improvements (and a private press screening to review a film about Milford), the New Plaza Theatre opened in January 1928, survived a flu epidemic and, by 1929, was advertising itself as "The House of Talkies."

Hanark Theatre | 1922–1927
(Newark)

The Hanark Theatre, owned by Louis Handloff, also held a name-this-theater contest. Unlike the Arcadia, which abandoned its own rules and picked the name it wanted, the Hanark opened without its name, billing itself simply as the New Theatre, until the permanent name was chosen. "Hanark" was a portmanteau of HANdloff (owner) and newARK (city). Unused suggestions included Cosey Corner, Delawana, Idle Hour and Cross Keys. The theater opened with D.W. Griffith's *Way Down East* and went on to host screenings for the American Legion, the United Jewish Campaign Relief Fund and the Women's Guild. In the fall of 1927, Handloff leased the building to the Atlantic and Pacific Tea Company and the theater closed.

Ringler's Theatre | 1923–1944
(Bethany Beach)

Built on Bethany Beach's boardwalk, Ringler's Theatre (a.k.a. the Bethany Theatre) was used heavily for community purposes, including commencement exercises, dances and high school basketball. Still, it was

This undated photo shows a haunting Ringler's Theatre on the distant, quiet boards of Bethany Beach. *Courtesy of the Town of Bethany Beach Cultural and Historical Affairs.*

a functioning movie theater and was available for theater parties, like the two-reeler hosted by the Delaware Safety Council in 1927.

State Theatre | 1929–1987
(Newark)

Louis Handloff, who had closed the Hanark in 1927, didn't waste much time before getting back into the business. In 1929, at 39 East Main Street, Handloff would open the State, a movie house with a seating capacity of seven hundred (five hundred downstairs, two hundred in the balcony). It was equipped with state-of-the-art twin Simplex film projectors and Vitaphone sound. (It was also designed for vaudeville and other stage productions.) Opening-night films were the short *That Certain Party* (a.k.a. *That Party in Person*) and the feature *Interference*.

MOVING PICTURES

The theatrical surge of the 1910s that carried into the start of the 1920s was evidenced by more than just a list of theaters. According to the *Morning News*, the Government Bureau of Home Economics published a report citing the typical Wilmington family of four spent an average of $11.71 *per year* on movies. That figure can barely get you a single ticket today, but in 1920, that was good enough for tops in the country for an entire year.

Theaters around the state took different approaches toward race. In the spring, the black community gathered at the National Theatre to reflect on three hundred years of people of color in the United States. But in the fall, George Schwartz, facing public pressure, reneged on contracts for the Negro Civic League to meet in both his Temple Theatre and Opera House in Dover. Schwartz later offered either one of the theaters to the League, but by that point, the League had notified members the meeting was canceled and declined Schwartz's offer. Adding insult to that, days after the Negro Civic League debacle, the Temple played host to what was billed as a "White Republican Rally"—a political event for white people only.

Fire was a routine occurrence at theaters in 1921, as no fewer than five places suffered some kind of damage or scare. The largest struck Georgetown in early January when a raging arson fire destroyed or damaged fourteen buildings, including Ryons Theatre, which, less than a year prior, had replaced the razed Peoples Theatre. At the Polonia, a projector's film magazine exploded; a month later, a circuit breaker blew at the Grand. In both cases, people were calmly evacuated, and in both cases, no real damage was done. At Dover's Temple Theatre, only slight water damage was done when a nearby store caught fire. The fifth fire occurred at the Palace in Milford.

There was a lot of change around the state leading into the middle of the decade. In 1922, Reese Harrington replaced the Reese Opera House with the Reese Theatre. In 1923, Wilmington's Polonia was sold at sheriff's sale (after having been sold at sheriff's sale earlier in the decade). In Dover, the Opera House was torn down to make way for a new and improved house. In Smyrna, the Citizens' Hose Company proposed taking over the Smyrna Opera House, which, according to the *Evening Journal*, was "now vacant for a club and recreation room." (The apparent closure of the Opera House approximately coincides with the opening of the Palace Theatre and/or that theater's change to the Strand; the Opera House appears to have remained closed until about 1930.) And fire destroyed Laurel's Waller Theatre, which would reopen a year later, almost to the day.

Things were looking better in Dover as the new Opera House was open and putting on the opera *Robin Hood* featuring the Dover Choral Society, and some special screenings were happening around the state. In 1927, the National

This is Reese Opera House and Reese Theatre proprietor Reese Harrington, around the time of the grand opening of the theater, which replaced the Opera House in 1922 after it had burned down. *Greater Harrington Historical Society.*

screened a newsreel exclusively comprising people of color. In 1928, the Dover Opera House had the opportunity to screen *40,000 Miles with Lindbergh*, a documentary (of sorts) about the life and travels of Charles Lindbergh, while the Ryons, which had survived the 1921 Georgetown fire, was showing *The World War*, a ten-reel picture about U.S. troops fighting in France.

The decade closed with a number of theaters moving to sound systems. In January, the Queen was equipped with Vitaphone and Movietone systems. (Later in the year, it would move to an all-talkie motion picture policy, then change systems again to an RCA Photophone.) In April, the Savoy would also upgrade to a Vitaphone system. In May, the Grand presented a "Grand Opening" (read: midnight screening) of the all-singing-dancing-talking revue *Fox Movietone Follies of 1929*; while in June, the Dover Opera House also made the audio tech upgrade scene, then doubled down in July with a new arc projector.

In business news, the end of the decade saw the Royal Theatre in New Castle become the Elaine, and the Dover Opera House was sold to Benjamin Shindler; George Schwartz subsequently wrote an open letter to Opera House investors stating he would personally oversee their repayment.

I think the Queen takes the prize for best screening of the decade, and that should be plural. First, in November 1921, the theater screened *A Romance of Wilmington*, shot on location and starring an amateur cast of locals, including Mayor LeRoy Harvey. Two years later, the theater would be the first in Wilmington to show footage of the Great Kantō Earthquake in Japan; only theaters in New York had shown the film first.

Topping all other stories in the 1920s was something sadly familiar. In April 1922, the Middletown Opera House burned down for the second time. This version of the Opera House had replaced the 1868 original, which had burned down in 1918. Fast-forward to déjà vu, even for the other tenants of the building, all of whom lost everything. The only good news to come out of the blaze was that even though the post office was completely destroyed, the postmaster, with help, managed to save the mail.

The plan in Middletown was to again rebuild, but with a twist. Gone forever was the Middletown Opera House, and some seven months later, the Everett Theatre was erected in its place. Named in honor of its owner, James Everett Lewis, the Everett Theatre opened on November 9, 1922, primarily as a movie house, with all the accoutrements of a modern theater, including eight hundred seats, plus twin Simplex projectors in its fireproof projection booth. The opening film was *Under Two Flags*, and the screening would be the first in a very, very long list of screenings to happen at the theater. That 1922 fire, though, wouldn't be the last time the theater would face adversity or closure.

CLOSING CREDITS

1914–1920: Victoria Theatre

A series of real estate moves signaled the beginning of the end of the Victoria. Due to a Wilmington Savings Fund Society project that called for the widening of Ninth Street between Market and King, the Victoria surrendered its lease. The owner had originally intended to move to a new location, but he decided to retire instead. The theater closed that March, but its furnishings would find their way to a new home: the Victory Theatre.

1908–1921: Pickwick Theatre

In January 1921, in Wilmington's fire-fearing environs, the Pickwick was closed by the city for lack of fire safety exits; city council deferred to the mayor to decide if the theater should reopen. I found no decision reported, but in April of that same year, the F.W. Woolworth Company signed a twenty-year lease on the building the Pickwick occupied, confirming the theater's fate.

Historic Movie Theaters of Delaware

1886–1923: Brandywine Springs Park Theatre

Although the park's theater stopped showing pictures in 1916, the park itself remained open until 1923. With the increase in personal automobile ownership allowing people greater flexibility, trolley usage dwindled, and with it dwindled interest in trolley parks.

1913–circa 1924: Palace Theatre | Nixon's Palace Theatre

In 1921, the Nixon-Nirdlinger syndicate purchased Milford's Palace Theatre, and remodeling began in May. In July of that same year, a fire in town damaged the Palace. Not long after, Nixon's Palace Theatre opened with modern projection equipment and six hundred seats. The theater appears to have closed for financial reasons, because in 1924, its fixtures were sold at a constable's sale in an effort recover past rent owed to the building's owner.

Films distributed by First National (Exhibitors' Circuit) were spotlighted for a week in February 1922 at Nixon's Palace Theatre in Milford. *In Old Kentucky* was co-produced by its star, Anita Stewart. *Delaware Public Archives, Dover, Delaware.*

Historic Movie Theaters of Delaware

Circa 1897–circa 1926: Coulbourn's Opera House

The last reference to Coulbourn's was about a dance in 1919, although a piece about the place being torn down in 1933 mentions the building had been condemned "several years ago." I split the difference between 1919 and 1933.

1911–1927: The Majestic Theatre

The Majestic was a participant in one key historic event and a witness to another in the 1920s. In 1922, Wilmington found itself the first city in the world to install wireless telephones for the purpose of reserving theater tickets. The Majestic was that theater, and the film was *Theodora*, a period drama set in ancient Rome.

Then, in September 1925, the theater screened a wrestling match between champ Ed "Strangler" Lewis and newcomer Wayne "Big" Munn. The event, which had occurred in January in Kansas City, landed on the big screen thanks to a cameraman who happened to hold the screen rights. What makes the match important in the history of professional wrestling is that wrestling historians look to this match as the first in the sport to be scripted. Early twentieth-century professional wrestling was traditional wrestling, but the matches became long and dull—so much so the sport was losing fans to boredom. Enter this contest, some entrepreneurialism and a shocking (and quick) match that reignited interest and turned a sport into entertainment.

The Majestic wouldn't last much longer after that. Just as the Pickwick had lost its space to Woolworth's, the Majestic, in 1927, lost its space to the Grant Company and its department store. The theater was given two weeks' notice to close. Its last screening was *Bertha, the Sewing Machine Girl*.

A postcard of the Majestic Theatre, 703½ Market Street, Wilmington. The Majestic was open from 1911 to 1927. *Delaware Public Archives, Dover, Delaware.*

Circa 1911–circa 1929: Wright's Theatre/Wright's Auditorium

A highlight for Wright's in 1921 was the live appearance of Little Miss Gwendolyn Letitia Jackson, a.k.a. Baby Gwendolyn. The child, at only five years of age, was a prodigy in chalk art and in demand at theaters around the region. This made her special enough, but the fact she was Jesse Wright's granddaughter made it extra-special. Over the remainder of the decade, the theater went through renovations and even survived a fire with minimal damage. In 1929, Jesse Wright attempted suicide. He had taken poison pills but was discovered by his wife and rushed to the hospital. He had already suffered two strokes and was forced to sell his businesses, including the theater. One year later, he succumbed to a third and fatal stroke.

SEEKING STARDOM

Hudson Theatre | circa 1920–circa 1930
(Selbyville)

The Hudson Theatre, a.k.a. Hudson's Theatre, first appears in July 1920 with an onstage marriage. Information is sparse over the next ten years and almost exclusively community-related. There is one mention in 1924 of a charity film screening that raised thirty dollars for local firefighters. It is possible this theater was also referred to as the Hudson Opera House and/or the Selbyville Theatre.

Dickerson Theatre | circa 1921
(Harrington)

In volume 20 of *Julius*, the Dickerson Theatre is listed as a movie house being managed by E.A. Wix, with a seating capacity of 250. Searches returned nothing else, and only one news item mentions an E.A. Wix in Harrington, albeit in the role of ice cream shop proprietor.

Milton Opera House | circa 1921
(Milton)

Just like the Dickerson Theatre, the Milton Opera House is listed in *Julius* volume 20 but found nowhere else. (In fact, *Julius* doesn't even list seating or management information.) It's possible this is another name for Milton's Fox Theatre, later named the Milton Theatre, but I could find no corroborating information to support that theory.

Millsboro Theatre | circa 1923
(Millsboro)

I came across this theater only once in a 1923 story about a KKK meeting there. One other website references a Millsboro Opera House but with no supporting evidence. I also discounted the possibility the intended reference was to the Ball Theatre, as that didn't open until 1938.

FADE OUT

It's almost as if the boom in sound technology created a whisper in theater openings. After years and years of boundless growth, the second half of the decade came to a near-halt in terms of new theater builds around the state. It also spelled the end to (or temporary interruption of) over a dozen theaters. Still, ending the decade with as many as forty-seven open theaters showed that while supply may have been leveling out, the demand was still high.

TAKE 6
THE 1930s

Slower, Lower

FADE IN

The slow growth experienced in the latter half of the 1920s continued to slog throughout the 1930s. Calculate into that more closures, and the result is a lower net theater count. Still, while the growth of new theaters may have stalled, that didn't mean theatrical activity slowed in any way. The 1930s were hectic all over the state.

OPENING CREDITS

Ball Theatre | 1938–circa 1974
(Millsboro)

It took most of the decade for the next new theater to come along in the state, but it was worth the wait, as the owner had perhaps the most unique background of any theater owner in the state's history. That owner was Walter M. Betts, who was, in certain circles, better known as Huck Betts. Millsboro born and raised, Betts, as a young boy, had a love and an affinity for baseball. In 1920, at the age of about twenty-three, Betts's skills were in demand, and he was signed to pitch for the Philadelphia Phillies. After six

Historic Movie Theaters of Delaware

WALTER (HUCK) BETTS
PITCHER, PHILADELPHIA NATIONALS

A baseball card of Ball Theatre owner Walter "Huck" Betts, from 1922, when he pitched with the Philadelphia Phillies. *From the author's personal collection.*

seasons with the Phils, followed by six seasons in the minors, he returned to The Show in 1932 with the Boston Braves and lasted four seasons, after which he retired and returned home, where soon after he opened the Ball Theatre on Main Street.

Warner Theatre | 1939–1977
(Wilmington)

It is impossible to say for sure if the Warner Theatre's 1939 opening was the most celebrated theater opening in the state's history, but it's at least in the conversation.

The notion of Wilmington having a full-blown Warner theater (not just a theater of another name owned by Warner Bros.) may have begun in 1930, when Pierre S. du Pont wrote a letter to Harry Warner asking for a theater to be built in Wilmington. Nine years later, it came to be. There was plenty of glitz and many big-name locals at 210 West Tenth Street on the evening of February 8, including Mayor Walter Bacon, Lieutenant Governor Edward Cooch and city council president Albert James. Mayor Bacon bought the first ticket, but the first real customer was John Steziska, age ten, who stood in line for hours to be the first. (But, you know, the mayor.) Also in attendance was Jack Warner Jr. of the Warner family.

When the Warner Theatre opened in Wilmington in 1939, a twenty-page program was available. The book, whose title page is featured here, contained information about the theater itself, brief bios of key theater players and congratulatory ads from Wilmington businesses. *Delaware Public Archives, Dover, Delaware.*

The $650,000 build was a two-year project in the making that made for the largest theater in the state. With 1,550 seats on the main floor and 350 in the loge, its capacity was already formidable, but the lobby had room for an additional 1,000 people, plus another 750 could fit in the foyer. From a tech perspective, the theater was state-of-the-art, with the same RCA Photophone equipment used at New York's Radio City Music Hall. The building also boasted year-round air conditioning, a first in the city.

Opening-night music was furnished by the bugle and drum corps of American Legion's Delaware Post 1, as flood lights and antiaircraft spotlights drew all the attention they could. Newsreel crews from Universal, Paramount and (of course) Warner Bros. were there to capture it all on film. The first feature was *Wings of the Navy*, accompanied by the short *Lincoln in the White House*.

The *News Journal* coverage on opening day was extensive, including a history of Warner Bros., a profile on theater manager Lewis Black, short entries written by Warner executives, a piece on the fashion found in *Wings of the Navy*, the audio equipment, the air conditioner and so on. Of course there were photos galore, as well as ads from countless contractors, local merchants and even other local theaters, all congratulating the Warner.

The day after the opening, the Warner took out a classy ad thanking the community for being so welcoming and apologizing to those who were unable to get in due to the crowds.

MOVING PICTURES

Slow growth may have been attributable to a leveling-off of customers, but you wouldn't know it by how many existing theaters hurried to upgrade to sound at the start of the decade. Theaters including the Strand, the Everett, the New and the Blue Hen all upgraded their equipment to screen talking pictures. Non-tech change was in the air at the start of the decade as well. The Dover Opera House held a contest to rename the theater (the winner was the Capital…or the Capitol—don't get me started); New Castle's Elaine, previously the Royal, was purchased by the Good Will Fire Company and renamed the Colonial. The Parkway, despite what appeared to be success with cooking and homemaking programs, was put up for sheriff's sale in the spring, and by fall, it had become an indoor miniature golf course and Wilmington's first indoor golf school. Warner Bros. came along and bought both the Grand (rebranding it the Grand Theatre) and the Savoy in Wilmington. It was also around this time downstate that the Fox Theatre became the Milton Theatre.

Fort DuPont began showing matinees on Sundays at the service club; these screenings would mark the first film matinees in the state's history. A year later, that same theater found itself in the middle of a measles epidemic, forcing it to forbid children under thirteen from entering. Scarlet fever kept the quarantine in effect until June. Late in the year, it was announced the army would build a four-hundred-seat theater dedicated to screening movies. This was meant to ease the burden of sharing the service hut, which was also used for dances and other social functions.

The fort wasn't the only place ready for change. Ryons Theatre in Georgetown underwent upgrades that included new projectors and sound machines, as well as new seats; it rebranded to become the Sussex Theatre. In Wilmington, Loew made its first acquisition in the city when it purchased the Parkway and upgraded all the projection and sound in the process. Management also installed a Transvox screen, something that was developed to help those seated closer to the side aisles have a

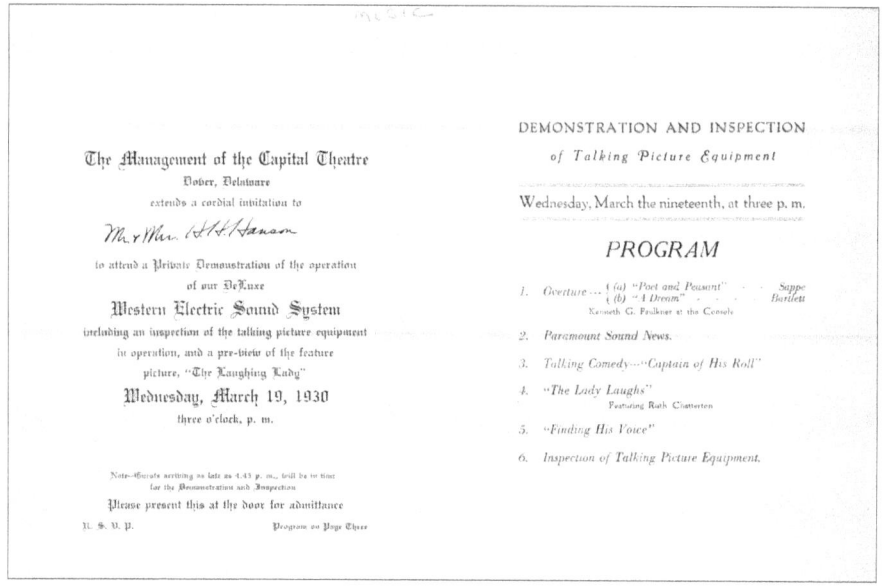

An invitation to a private demonstration of a new sound system at the Capitol Theatre in 1930. Based on the program, it appears a full evening's moving picture viewing was on the docket, followed by a chance to see the equipment up close. *Delaware Public Archives, Dover, Delaware.*

more center row–like viewing experience. Joining the sound revolution were Newark's State Theatre and Dover's Temple Theatre.

Other theaters seeing action in 1931 included Keller's, which was put up for sale; the National, which suffered considerable damage when fire at a nearby stable spread; and the Smyrna Opera House, which suddenly resurrected as the Como Theatre after years of being dormant. Also back on the scene was George Schwartz, who returned to the Dover Opera House, and New Castle's recently renamed Colonial became the Earle. In 1932, the Everett closed, was put up for sheriff's sale in 1933 and bought by George Schwartz in 1934. Also, Seaford's New Theatre changed hands and became the Palace; it changed hands again when it, along with the Sussex Theatre, was purchased by Thomas Ayers. More theaters boarded the sound train, too. The Avenue became the first theater in the state to have installed RCA's "High Fidelity" sound system. The Park Theatre was also the recipient of a new sound system: Wide Range, developed by Bell Telephone Laboratories and courtesy of Western Electric. And after delays, Uncle Sam finally opened that four-hundred-seat Fort DuPont theater (sometimes known as the War Department Theatre).

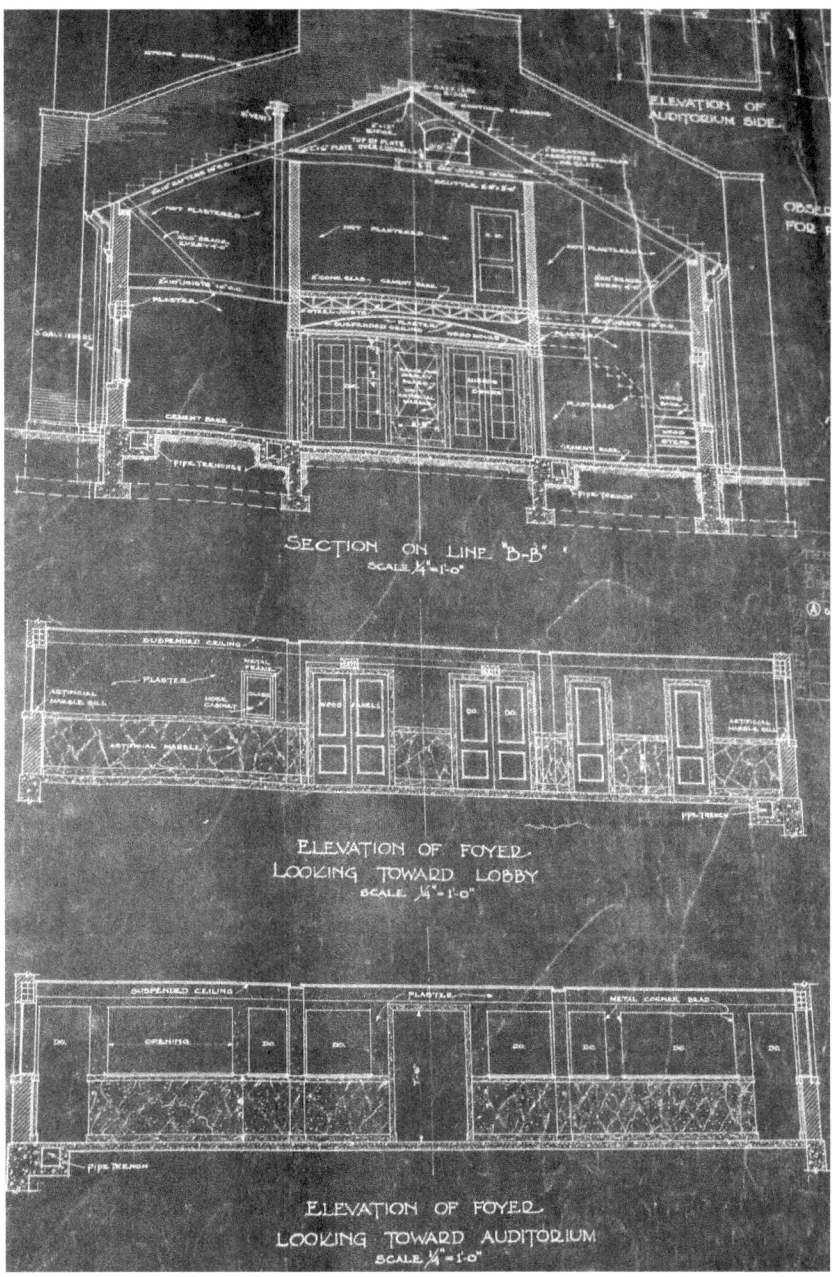

This portion of original blueprints from the theater at Fort DuPont illustrates the building entrance and foyer. A collection of original blueprints is part of the Fort DuPont archives. *Delaware State Parks, Cultural Resources Unit.*

In Wilmington, blue laws again were strained against. In October 1934, Loew's was to have hosted a special Sunday screening for seven hundred people who had contributed to a benefit fund for the Homeopathic Hospital. Mayor Speer warned the theater manager that screening a film on Sunday would result in a loss of license on Monday. The theater held its screening at midnight, but not many guests had remained. In other morality-themed, troubled-screening news, the Catholic Church boycotted theaters because of the content and quality of films being played. This boycott was forcing many independently owned theaters to temporarily close.

In May 1935, after seven years of having been used mostly for comunity functions, Delmar's Elcora Theatre returned to life under the Delmar Theatre moniker, while Seaford's Palace Theatre burned down just days before Christmas. Owner Thomas Ayers vowed to rebuild the Palace, and rebuild it he did in April 1936 (keeping the same name). Not all names remained the same, though. In addition to the Como in Smyrna becoming the Roxy, the Avenue in Wilmington, which had already existed as the Polonia, changed names again, but this time it turned to its patrons to assist with the renaming, offering five dollars cash for the winning entry. That winning entry was the Ace Theatre. In addition to getting a new name, the theater also had installed an RCA Sonotone system, which offered hearing aids to those in need so the wonder known as talking pictures could be enjoyed by all.

Unique screenings dominated 1938 stories. Claymont's Green Lantern screened a film called *Forbidden*, which was touted as showing actual childbirth. Screenings were adults only, with a "Nurse in Attendance at All Shows!" The screenings were also divided by gender so that only men were admitted to certain screenings while only women were admitted to others. Also at the Green Lantern were exploitation films like *Smashing the Vice Trust*, *Marijuana Madness* and *Race Suicide*. In other news, the Milton Theatre caught fire and sustained considerable damage.

There was an interesting legal item of note in 1938 involving Laurel's Waller Theatre. Popular in 1930s movie houses around the country (including the Roxy and the Blue Hen) was something called Bank Night. It was a lottery of sorts that promised cash prizes to patrons whose names (or designated numbers) were drawn. If no one claimed their prize, that money went toward the next drawing, and so on. Bank Night was trademarked and run nationally (with the founding organization getting its cut from each theater, of course). Roland Waller had originally signed a deal with Affiliated Enterprises Inc. for Bank Night to be run in his theater, but when questions

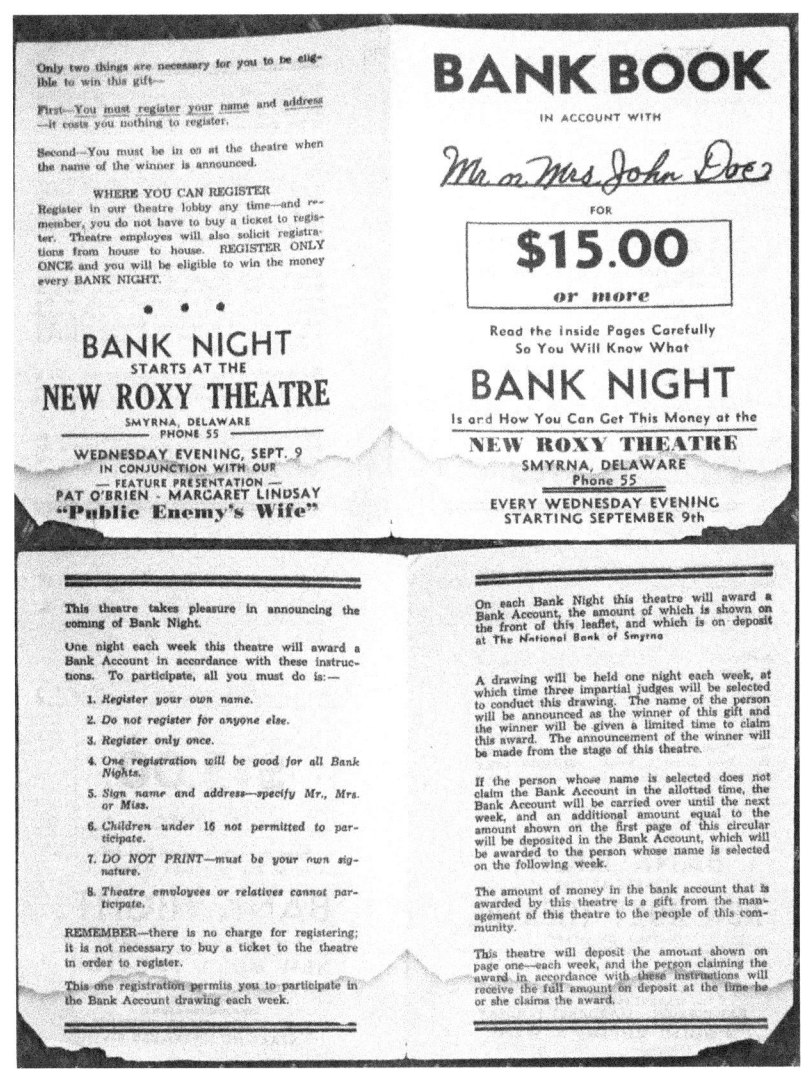

This is an example of a "Bank Book" theaters used when Bank Nights were popular in the 1930s. This particular book was used at the Roxy in 1936. Bank Nights were deemed illegal in the state in 1939. The book is now part of the Smyrna Opera House archives. *Courtesy of Smyrna Opera House.*

of the legality of the game were raised, Waller abandoned his plan. Affiliate Enterprises sued for breach of contract, but that turned costly for them. The case would carry over into 1939 when the issue of the general legality of Bank Nights was raised, and the court found the entire practice to be illegal. This ruling ended Bank Nights in Delaware.

But the biggest story of 1939 may have come out of Rehoboth: the story of the Blue Hen and the blue laws.

On Sunday, July 31, the Blue Hen screened *It Could Happen to You*, a harmless comedy/mystery from 20th Century Fox. Despite blue laws—laws that prohibited "worldly labor" on the Sabbath—having been on the books in Delaware since 1794, the Blue Hen had been showing movies on Sundays (in-season) the previous four years and had done so openly. But something about 1939 had people ready to rise up, including politicians, preachers and protestors. A complaint was filed, and theater owner Charles S. Horn pleaded guilty and paid a fine of four dollars.

Locals in Rehoboth wanted exemptions for in-season Sundays for fear that Maryland theaters not bound by blue laws would take away business and hurt the resort town's economy. A bill had even been passed by both of Delaware's legislative houses the previous spring, but it was vetoed by Governor Richard McMullen.

On Sunday, August 6, Horn, despite his arrest and fine from the previous week, and despite warnings from the deputy attorney general, screened another film. Again he was fined. The Sunday after that, Horn defied the law again, and for the third time he was fined, although this time, three employees were fined as well.

Horn's legal strategy was to draw attention to the outdated laws by forcing officials to make enforcement strict. His attorney argued that other merchants working on Sundays, including grocery stores and gas stations, were also in violation of the law but none was being targeted by officials. The strategy worked. Politicians and religious leaders across the state concurred it was both unfair to target one business over any other and that the laws of so long ago should be revisited to be practical in a modern society. As Horn continued to defy the law as it was written, and as his lawyer continued to press for full enforcement for all Sunday violators, pressure mounted on politicians.

CLOSING CREDITS

1903–1930: Garrick Theatre

On June 7, 1930, after screening *The Royal Rider*, the Garrick closed. It had only ever shown silent pictures.

Historic Movie Theaters of Delaware

1920–1930: Frankford Opera House

When I used to think about the dawn of sound and film exhibition, I only ever considered the positives. For the Frankford Opera House, the sound era did not mean a tech upgrade, it meant the end. Unable to afford the equipment to show sound pictures, Clarence T. Esham and Russell Jones, who had assumed operation of the Opera House and the latter of whom was the son of retired owner Benjamin Jones, were forced to close.

1920–1930: Victory Theatre | Hunt's Theatre | Broadway Theatre

Some records suggest the Victory closed in 1929 when its manager, A.J. DeFiore, resigned to become manager of the Park Theatre. There is evidence, though, to suggest the theater was open in 1930, but after that it was closed for two years before being sold and reopened as a meeting place for the Sons of Italy.

Circa 1919–circa 1930: Dodd's Hall

A children's minstrel show in 1930 was the last item I found on Dodd's, although in 1990, John W. Tingle passed away, and in his obituary was listed his past job as a projectionist at Dodd's when he was nine years old. He would go on to be a projectionist at the Ball and the Clayton.

Circa 1872–circa 1931: Milford Opera House

I was unable to confirm the close year of the Milford Opera House. I found one mention in 1931 when it hosted the Junior Order of United American Mechanics. The group screened films of the orphanages the order sponsored.

1885–circa 1933: Caskey Hall | Newark Opera House

I found almost nothing on the Newark Opera House in the 1930s, either. The latest event I found was a Pentecostal revival in November 1933. In July 1934, it was up for sheriff's sale. It became apartments sometime in the 1930s.

HISTORIC MOVIE THEATERS OF DELAWARE

1892–1934: Shellpot Park Theatre

Although the park stopped showing films in 1917, it still provided entertainment to families until 1934, when it burned down.

SEEKING STARDOM

Robin Hood Theatre | 1931–1969
Candlelight Music Dinner Theatre | 1969-2004
New Candlelight Theatre | 2004–2014
Candlelight Theatre | 2014–present
(Wilmington)

The first new theater to be christened in the 1930s was interesting to designate as Seeking Stardom because a lot is known about the entity, and it is still in business as of this writing; ultimately, I placed it in this section because the history of film here is slight. The Robin Hood Theatre made its debut in June 1931 with the play *The First and Last*, and for decades its specialty was live theater. In the 1960s, with attendance waning, it added films to its regular schedule (the first was *Show Boat*). Despite showcasing films by Charlie Chaplin and W.C. Fields, and even after briefly jettisoning live performances entirely in exchange for double features, the Robin Hood couldn't draw. It would suffer temporary closures over time, and today, now long-removed from its dalliances with film, it stays true to its roots and showcases live performances.

Pierce's Theatre | circa 1936
(Bethany Beach)

In the mid-1920s, the Tunnells, a family closely identified with lower Delaware's business and social scenes, began a tradition of holding family reunions in Bethany. Normally, they would convene at Ringler's Theatre, but in 1936, the clan reunited at Pierce's Theatre (a.k.a. Pierce Theatre), also in Bethany. What's curious is I could find no reason as to why they changed venues, and aside from the photo here and three articles about that reunion that specific year, I found no other references to the Pierce's Theatre.

Dozens of Tunnell family members gathered at Pierce's Theatre in Bethany in 1936 for their annual family reunion. This was a departure from their traditional gathering spot of Ringler's Theatre, also in Bethany. *Delaware Public Archives, Dover, Delaware.*

Diamond Theatre | 1937–1955, 1959–1960
(Selbyville)

The Diamond Theatre in Selbyville is another that was difficult to classify. It was built in 1937 by Raymond T. Quillin of Berlin, Maryland, who already had had theater experience as owner of the Globe Theater in Berlin in 1926. While the Diamond would be one of seventeen theaters statewide to take part in the Fifth War Loan Bond sales in the 1940s, it otherwise remained obscure. It closed and reopened in the 1950s, only to close for good in 1960.

FADE OUT

From the close of the 1920s to the close of the 1930s, Delaware's theater count had dropped by a net of five, to forty-one (after having dipped to thirty-eight during the decade). But the theme of the decade wasn't so much about quantity as it was quality, with advances in the field of sound technology, the birth of the Warner and the fight for movies on Sundays. Little did anyone know then what was in store for the Delaware theater scene in the 1940s.

War.

And drive-ins.

LOST AND FOUND

Lost theater memories can be found around the state if you know where to look.

This is an original Reese Theatre student pass from 1939, available to view at the Greater Harrington Historical Society. *Photo by Victoria Nazarewycz.*

TAKE 7
THE 1940s

Powers, Allied

FADE IN

The 1940s would bounce back to late-1920s levels of theater volume, aided mostly by a flat closure rate of existing theaters, spikes in openings in the early and late parts of the decade and the dawn of Delaware's drive-in era. Packed with many smaller stories, the decade would also show a considerable legal shift in film exhibition and an unprecedented unity among theaters in response to World War II.

OPENING CREDITS

Layton Theatre | 1941–1982
Layton Cinema | 1982–1984
(Seaford)

With Seaford's Palace Theatre turning twenty years old, owner Thomas Ayers was ready to offer the town a new theater for live shows and movies. At the corner of Pennsylvania Avenue and Shipley Street, Ayers built the eight-hundred-seat Layton Theatre, named after his son. Prominent Delawareans, including Governor Walter Bacon, were invited to the grand opening. The first film screened was the Hal Roach comedy *Road Show*.

One of the theater's first-year highlights was an appearance and speech by famed explorer Admiral Richard Byrd. Over the course of the decade, the Layton proved itself to be a bedrock of the community, hosting fundraisers for various social and women's organizations, providing charity screenings for underprivileged kids and joining war efforts by hosting salvage drives, sailor relief fund screenings and bond sales.

Delmar Drive-In (1) | 1941–circa 1946
(Delmar)

In my notes, I have always referred to this theater as "Delmar Drive-In (1)," located on Laurel-Delmar Highway, because there is a second, unaffiliated Delmar Drive-In that opened in 1950 on Bi-State Boulevard ("Delmar Drive-In (2)," of course). I cannot ascertain the actual name of Delmar Drive-In (1), as any printed resources I have seen refer to the theater in generic terms: "Drive-In Theatre," "Open Air Movies," "Drive-In Movies" and so on.

The theater opened in June 1941, it played films and hosted live shows and it (adorably) advertised that the films were free but the parking cost money (twenty-five to fifty cents per car). There are a handful of newspaper advertisements that confirm it was open at least in the summers of 1941 and 1942, and while some sources date the theater's close around 1943, there is a news item related to the Delmar Drive-In (2) that suggests the close year for (1) was closer to 1946. The most pertinent point, though, is that all of this establishes the Delmar Drive-In (1) as Delaware's first drive-in theater, a title commonly thought to be held by the Brandywine Drive-In (later in this chapter).

Avenue Theatre | 1941–1962
(Rehoboth Beach)

Situated at 32 Rehoboth Avenue, the Avenue Theatre could seat 458 people downstairs and another 96 in the balcony, it had the latest in A/V equipment, it was air conditioned throughout and in it William Derrickson planned to show first-run pictures (but only at night, unless rain thwarted vacationers' outdoor plans). For its part in the war effort, the theater helped raise money for the Red Cross and sold war bonds; it also allowed WAC officers to speak to its audiences in a recruiting effort and was an official collection center for the Victory Book Campaign, which helped collect books to send to troops.

Edge Moor Theatre | 1941–1980
(Wilmington)

Located on Governor Printz Boulevard at Edge Moor Terrace, the three-story, 850-seat Edge Moor Theatre (also known as the Edgemoor Theatre) was one part of a larger shopping and residential complex, the plans for which included a department store, a restaurant, apartments and shops. On November 26, one day after an invitation-only private screening of *It Started with Eve* (followed by a reception at the Hotel du Pont), the theater opened to the public with the comedy *Nothing but the Truth*. Not long after the theater opened, Pearl Harbor was attacked. Shortly after that, the theater was used for civil defense recruiting in the community. The theater also participated in bond sales throughout the decade.

The Theater at Dover Air Force Base | circa 1941–present
(Dover)

Dover AFB's theater was another located on a Delaware military base. The history of the base itself begins in 1939, when the U.S. government looked to shore up its coasts with airfields after the Nazis invaded Poland; the base went into action after the bombing of Pearl Harbor. Not long after, a movie theater, which doubled as a chapel, was added. An incarnation of that theater still exists today.

When first constructed in 1941, the theater at the Dover Air Force Base also doubled as a chapel. In this photo from August 29, 1943, the comedic double feature was *Here Comes Kelly* and *Honeymoon Lodge*. The former had yet to be released to the public, something not uncommon for screenings at DAFB. *Delaware Public Archives, Dover, Delaware.*

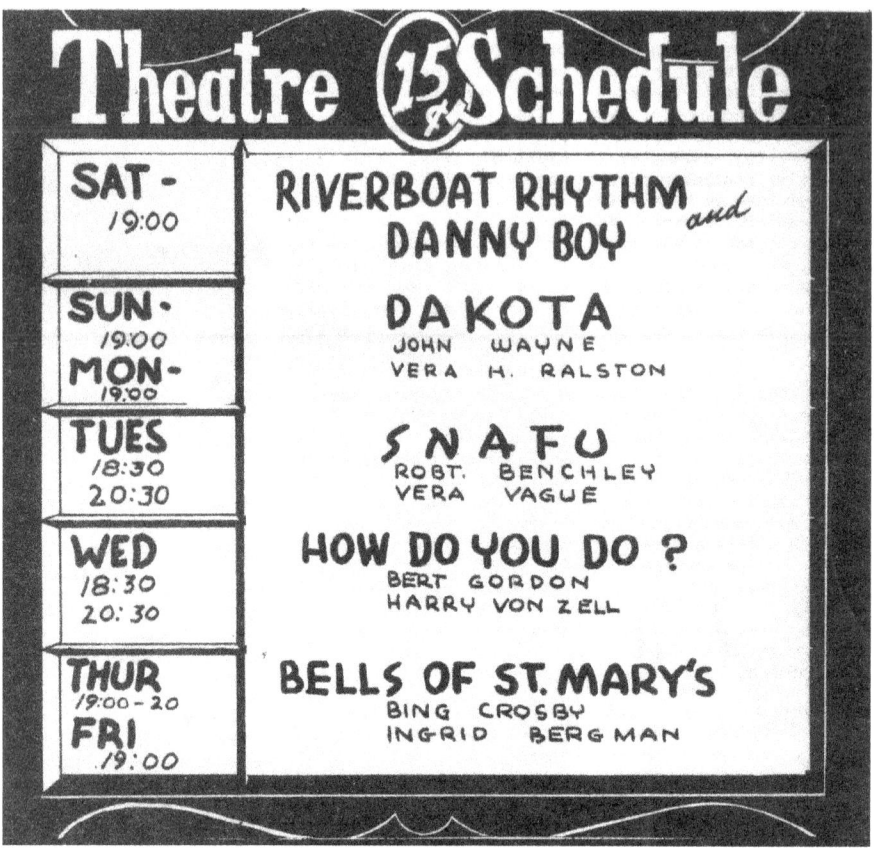

This film schedule appeared in the December 14, 1945 edition of the Dover Air Force Base newspaper, the *Dover Blast*. Each of these films were new releases. *AMC Museum.*

The Theater at New Castle Army Air Base | circa 1941–1946 (New Castle)

Another on-base theater to open around the same time as Dover AFB and Fort Miles was housed at New Castle's Army Air Base. Its existence was short-lived, with little information readily available, although the base took part in bond sales, including an event in 1943 where the base's Jive Bombers Orchestra (what a name!) played a gig at Sixth and Market Streets in Wilmington, where Hollywood star Dean Jagger (*White Christmas*) was making an appearance. After World War II was over, personnel were reassigned and parts of the base were shuttered, including the theater.

Historic Movie Theaters of Delaware

The Theater at Fort Miles | 1942–1963
(Lewes)

A fourth on-base theater was found at the other end of the state, at Fort Miles. The base itself was established in 1941; in March 1942, sponsored by a "coordinating committee" comprising members of the USO and the Red Cross, the three-hundred-seat theater (plus rec hall) was opened for the use of personnel on the base. Later that year, air conditioning was added. The theater participated in war bond sales, and in addition to films, both parties and dances were held there, as were live shows put on by soldiers. Postwar, there was a second theater on the base, but I consider them a singular entity.

Crest Theatre | 1942–1960
(Wilmington)

Those who attended the grand opening of the 780-seat Crest were greeted by usherettes before they were treated to Alfred Hitchcock's *Suspicion*. The theater, located at Maryland Avenue and Boxwood Road, offered air conditioning, free parking and standing room behind the last row of seats in the event of a large crowd. It, too, participated in scrap drives and war bond sales. For its community, the Crest frequently availed itself for Sunday church usage. In the summer of 1945, it scheduled special children's matinees to keep kids out of trouble in the heat, and in the summer of 1946, it hosted a series of children's talent shows for cash prizes.

Center Theatre | 1946–1978
(Rehoboth Beach)

Four years would pass before the next theater opened in the state, via William Derrickson, who continued to grow his beach business with the addition of the Center Theatre at 41 Rehoboth Avenue, not far from his Avenue Theatre. Mayor Edgar Stayer attended the November grand opening; it was the third open theater in the resort town.

Sidney Theatre | 1948–1961
(Bridgeville)

In the same decade William Derrickson opened his second theater, Thomas Ayers opened his fourth. Seven years after Keller's Theatre burned down, Bridgeville had a new theater: the Sidney, located at the corner of Laws Street and Delaware Avenue. As its opening screening on May 6, the theater chose *Glamour Girl*.

Clayton Theatre | 1949–present
(Dagsboro)

With Governor Elbert Carvel in attendance and a performance by the John M. Clayton School Band preceding its opening screening, the Clayton Theatre—the first theater in Dagsboro's history—raised its curtain and rolled its projectors (showing *One Touch of Venus*) on February 2. The concrete art deco theater, built by Alvin "Skeet" Campbell; his wife, Marjorie; his brother-in-law Elwood "Pete" Hancock; and Pete's wife, Marian, was so popular, on opening night, the doors were torn from their hinges due to the rush of patrons.

Manor Theatre | 1949–1957
(New Castle)

On June 3, 1949, at DuPont Boulevard and Franklin Avenue, in the Wilmington Manor section of New Castle, the Manor Theatre held its grand opening, with news, cartoons, shorts and the main feature, MGM's star-studded *Little Women*. For Christmas, the Wilmington Manor Lions Club entertained over 400 in the 480-seat theater. Cartoons were on the reels, with candy and gifts given to all.

Brandywine Drive-In | 1949–1955
Ellis Drive-In | 1955–circa 1977
(New Castle)

Set to be Delaware's first postwar drive-in (and the state's lone drive-in at the time, at least for a month), the Brandywine Drive-In opened on July

15 to such a turnout that despite being able to accommodate 1,150 cars, hundreds more were turned away. Located one mile south of Wilmington on DuPont Highway, the Brandywine opened with Errol Flynn in *The Adventures of Robin Hood*.

Diamond State Drive-In | 1949–1973
Hiway 13 Drive-In | 1973–circa 1985
Diamond State Drive-In | 1986, 1995–2008
(Felton)

On South DuPont Highway in Felton, Mildred and Albert Steele opened Delaware's next drive-in, the two-hundred-car Diamond State. For their first season, they had no sound boxes to hang from car windows. Instead, three horn speakers sat atop the sixty-by-forty-foot screen and piped sound toward the cars (and for another two to three miles beyond that).

MOVING PICTURES

It is difficult to encapsulate on a linear timeline the goings-on in the state in the 1940s. Where past decades had singular moments or years that are easy to pluck and point to as a section-ending highlight, this decade's small stories are numerous and scattered, and its big stories are years-spanning.

Before any new theater would open in the state in the 1940s, one of the greatest movies of all time would open first. *Gone with the Wind* had three U.S. premieres in December 1939: Atlanta (12/15), New York (12/19), and Los Angeles (12/28). It saw its general release on January 17, 1940, and the Loew's Parkway was the first Wilmington theater to screen the film (and as best as I can tell, the first theater in Delaware) beginning on January 26. Anticipation for the film was so high, Loew's sold tickets in advance (even by mail), and for evening shows, the theater offered reserved seating. Tickets were $0.75 for the matinee and $1.10 for the evening. The Wilmington premiere was quite an event, too. Most of the 1,000-plus attendees, including members of Delaware society and politics, were in formal attire, along with 130 southerners brought in for the screening. Another 40 girls were dressed as belles, a live band played Dixieland music and Confederate flags hung outside the theater.

SCHINE'S NEW
PLAZA THEATRE
MILFORD
ENTIRE WEEK OF MARCH 11ᵀᴴ

DAVID O. SELZNICK'S
production of
MARGARET MITCHELL'S
Story of the Old South

GONE WITH THE WIND

IN TECHNICOLOR, *starring*
CLARK GABLE
as Rhett Butler
LESLIE   OLIVIA
HOWARD · de HAVILLAND
and presenting
VIVIEN LEIGH
as Scarlett O'Hara
A SELZNICK INTERNATIONAL PICTURE
Directed by VICTOR FLEMING
Screen Play by Sidney Howard
Music by Max Steiner
A Metro-Goldwyn-Mayer Release

Left: Most likely from 1940, this undated program is for a weeklong screening run of *Gone with the Wind* (1939) at Milford's Plaza Theatre. *Milford Museum Collection.*

Below: The State Theatre, 39 East Main Street, Newark, circa 1940. *Photo by Leo Laskaris, courtesy of the Newark Historical Society.*

Around the state in 1940, Laurel's Waller Theatre burned down, but owner R.H. Waller had designs on rebuilding (which he would do the following year). In Claymont, the Green Lantern became the Don Theatre (only to be renamed the Pike a year later), and in Newark, the State Theatre upgraded its projection and sound equipment to keep up with Hollywood technology.

It was also a busy year in 1941. In Wilmington, something of a trade was made. Warner purchased the Parkway from Loew's and renamed it the Ritz, while at the same time Loew's took over the Aldine and renamed it Loew's Aldine. In Georgetown, the Sussex Theatre suffered complete interior damage when a short circuit caused a blaze in April (with a second fire adding insult to injury in June). It would be rebuilt and reopen in November as the Ayers Theatre. The year was also about the armed forces. In Lewes, an influx of servicemen who were allowed to leave their encampments to go into town each night gave the Lewes Auditorium the idea to open every night of the week, all summer, to accommodate them. Later that summer, all Warner theaters in Wilmington reduced their prices for servicemen.

Sad news came in August 1942 when George Schwartz died unexpectedly at the age of fifty. His theater business, which included the Capitol and Temple in Dover, the Strand in Smyrna and the Everett in Middletown, would continue to be run by his widow, Reba, and his daughter, Muriel.

In the early morning hours of November 15, 1943, Harrington's Reese Theatre caught fire. Four hours later, only the walls of the building remained. Reese Harrington intended to rebuild. And in 1944, the Delmar suffered fire damage to the stage and screen; it would be remodeled as part of the recovery effort.

In 1945, President Roosevelt passed away. All Warner theaters in the city closed for his funeral.

That same year, in Harrington, the new Reese Theatre opened, billing itself as "The Movie Center of Delaware and Maryland." The grand opening featured *Christmas in Connecticut* as its first film. The theater boasted several unique offerings beyond the usual audio/visual fare, including a crying room for mothers with fussy babies, Sonophone devices for the hearing impaired and something called the Rainbow Room, available for screening parties that wanted some sense of privacy. The theater also offered a manned parcel check room for patrons who took in a movie after shopping.

In 1946, with World War II in the rear-view mirror, theater activity reverted to prewar levels and themes. St. John's Roman Catholic Church

In 1946, the Temple Theatre in Dover screened *Conquest of Cheyenne*, starring Wild Bill Elliott as Red Ryder, a western hero first made popular in comic strips. This was the same Red Ryder whose BB gun Ralphie was so eager to get in the 1983 film *A Christmas Story*. *Delaware Public Archives, Dover, Delaware.*

sponsored a screening of *The Song of Bernadette* at the State Theatre, while at the Pike, the local American Legion post hosted a benefit screening where the cost for one ticket was one canned good. Things were a little flashier in Wilmington, where Albert and Jack Warner, two of the Warner brothers, were in town to celebrate the twentieth anniversary of sound in motion pictures (WB's *Don Juan*, from 1926). The brothers visited all the city's Warner properties: the Warner, Grand, Arcadia, Ritz, Queen and Savoy. Flashy for other reasons was a visit to the city by Nancy Hartung, the first female film rep to come to town. She was promoting *Caesar and Cleopatra*.

Also flashy was Hollywood star Robert Cummings's visit to the town of Delmar in 1946. Mrs. Robert Vincent was one of forty-two thousand radio contest entrants to explain how she would spend a day with the star: she would have Cummings help her and her husband run their grocery store. That was the winning answer. Cummings arrived in Salisbury to a crowd of about one thousand people and spent the day with the Vincents, including

This incarnation of the Reese Theatre replaced the Reese Opera House in 1922 and lasted until it burned down in 1943. The photo is undated. *Greater Harrington Historical Society.*

This is the Reese Theatre as it was rebuilt after the 1943 fire. This photo is from around 1945. *Greater Harrington Historical Society.*

lunch out, dinner at their apartment and, yes, clerking in their store. All of this happened on the Maryland side of Delmar, but the day ended in Delaware, where the Vincents, Cummings and others screened *The Bride Wore Boots*, starring Cummings and Barbara Stanwyck. The screening occurred at the Avenue Theatre, built earlier in the year to replace the burned-down Delmar Theatre.

The Strand Theatre, which went dark in 1945, was replaced by the adjacent Smyrna Theatre in April 1948. A private affair at the theater for 250 guests, hosted by Reba and Muriel Schwartz, included Governor Bacon. The theater seated 600 and included in the building a soda shop, a nursery and a "hunt room" for private parties.

At the Ace in Wilmington, the once family- and church-friendly theater found itself on the receiving end of a one-year Catholic boycott for screening the film *Mom and Dad*, which the church's Legion of Decency had rated as "Condemned." [The film's IMDbPro description: "Because a high school girl's parents refuse to discuss sex education (called 'personal hygiene' in the film) with her, she gets pregnant by her boyfriend, who conveniently dies. Her parents are blamed, and the local sex education teacher uses this opportunity to show a film showing the dangers (and results) of VD and the birth of a baby."]

This is an architect's sketch of what would become the Smyrna Theatre. *Delaware Public Archives, Dover, Delaware.*

And on April 2, 1948, the architect's vision became reality. *Courtesy of the Duck Creek Historical Society.*

The Ace's initial response to the boycott seemed frantic. It cited that while the film did not meet with Catholic approval, it had been screened and endorsed by many youth organizations, including the Boy Scouts and the YMCA. The theater also stated it had attempted to cancel the rental of the film upon hearing of the Catholic disapproval but was threatened with a lawsuit by producers if the film was not played. In advertisements, the Ace attempted to counter the Legion's boycott by reinforcing its approval by many other groups (including generic "clergy") and by printing pull-quotes as a testament to the film's importance.

The theater held gender-specific screenings, and while the women's opening night screening saw no attendance issues, so many men grew impatient to get into the theater for their later showing the theater's doors were smashed. A month or so later, the Legion's boycott was called off after coming to the agreement that the theater would "show in the future none but pictures approved by the Legion."

On Christmas night 1948, Smyrna's Roxy was decimated by fire, and the building would sit unused for its intended purpose for the next fifty years. With little happening in 1949, this fire was a tough way to end the 1940s.

Looking back on the decade, where others had one or two big stories that were relatively well contained, the 1940s had three massive stories—one local, one statewide and one with national impact.

The third-biggest story of the decade, the local story, began in 1946 with a large fire and ended with an even larger antitrust lawsuit.

On September 23, around 1:00 a.m., a fire broke out in the New Plaza Theatre in Milford, and within an hour, the building was completely gutted; fire companies from ten nearby towns raced to assist Milford firemen. Executives from Schine Chain Theatres Inc., the largest independent theater circuit in the country at the time and owners of the theater, were on the scene the next day, along with Milford mayor Edward Evans, who also was the manager of the theater. Within a week, the decision had been made to rebuild on the same spot. About two weeks later, it was announced that Schine had reached an agreement with Milford's Carlisle Fire Company to use the gymnasium in the community building to screen films while the new theater was being constructed. The theater chain would pay to remodel the gym and add soundproofing. This interim theater would be known as the Community Plaza Theatre.

Two weeks after that, on October 28, Milford was treated to the opening of what would have been its second movie theater, the Shore Theatre, located in what used to be Armory Hall. Guests at the opening-night festivities included Mayor Evans. The following month, Schine doubled down on its rebuild by purchasing the land adjacent to the original theater with the intent of building larger than before.

Then, in March 1947, the owner of the Shore Theatre filed an antitrust lawsuit against Schine. But Schine wasn't the only defendant. Also part of the suit were the following motion picture producers: Columbia, Loew's, Paramount, RKO, Republic, 20th Century Fox, United Artists, Universal and Warner Bros. According to the *Morning News*, Shore charged that the Schine Plaza "received preferential treatment from the defendant distributors, even after [it] burned to the ground…and was later set up in the back of a fire house." Shore also claimed "it was required to pay discriminatory film rentals substantially in excess of those charged Schine for like pictures in comparable theatres." In addition to "competitive disadvantage," the suit also alleged several other things: that Schine had attempted to buy the Shore Theatre, but in failing to do so, then prevented the Shore from accessing suitable films; that this happened even though the Shore was the lone movie house in Milford, especially when compared to the "make-shift theater" Schine ran; and that prior to the Schine Plaza having burned down, it changed its programming three times a week, but while in the fire house, it changed its programming four times a week. According to the plaintiff, all of this forced Shore to screen mostly older pictures, reissues or "inferior pictures of lesser distributors 'not made parties to this action.'" All of this was alleged to have happened while the Shore had 500 seats and Schine's Community Plaza Theatre had only 325.

Cutting through the rest of the legalese, Shore sought to prevent Schine from receiving an excessive number of films, thus denying the Shore access to the same; to ensure film rentals to the Shore were competitive; and to ensure the Shore was not discriminated against when it came to renting films. The suit would take years.

In July 1947, Schine Plaza manager (and Milford mayor) Edward Evans resigned from his theater management duties. He had been with the theater for twenty years, starting as a projectionist and staying on as manager when Schine took over the theater. He cited as the reason for his departure his desire to focus his non-mayoral time on the new restaurant he opened after the theater fire. Meanwhile, the build of the new theater continued, and in 1948, the Milford Theatre opened with a dedication parade and a screening of *The Fuller Brush Man*.

Schine's Milford Theatre, circa 1949. *Milford Museum Collection.*

The second-biggest story of the year was statewide. On March 14, 1941, after endless months of political machinations, Governor Bacon signed a repeal of the two-hundred-year-old blue law—a repeal that passed by a margin of 18–16 in the House and 13–3 in the Senate and would legally permit theaters in incorporated cities and towns to show movies on Sundays (between noon and 6:00 p.m. and between 8:00 p.m. and midnight). However, towns also had the right make their own local rules, something that would happen around the state, including later the same year, when residents of Newark petitioned to ban movies on Sundays, a move that would have directly affected the State Theatre. People protested the first Sunday screening at the Earle Theatre (a slightly different case, since New Castle still needed its own referendum to allow Sabbath screenings).

In 1942, with the state repeal of the dated legislation, the Lewes Auditorium was set to show its first Sunday picture in May. But in response to opposition from two evangelical leaders, town commissioners passed a resolution banning Sunday movies, but they did so without a town referendum. On November 24, 1946, some four years after town commissioners took matters out of the people's hands, the residents of Lewes took matters back and voted 184–97 in favor of allowing movies on Sundays.

Meanwhile, in 1949, the Clayton, which had opened in February and was showing movies six nights per week, took charge and polled the community, and a referendum was held. In an 88–34 vote, the community granted permission for Sunday movies; the Clayton gladly obliged beginning on October 16. That same year, Middletown also passed its own referendum, 337–114, to allow the Everett to show movies on Sundays.

But the biggest statewide story in the 1940s, the one borne of national (and international, really) events and one of the biggest stories in the history of Delaware theaters, occurred after the bombing of Pearl Harbor in December 1941, when theaters' social focus pivoted, and efforts to help the community became efforts to rally the community to help the war effort.

To aid in that effort, the State Theatre was one of many Newark businesses collecting scrap, as did Milford's New Plaza Theatre. At the Ball Theatre, tin cans from boys and rags from girls earned children matinee tickets. The Warner held a "rubber day" matinee, collecting four thousand pounds of the stuff from over one thousand kids, with items redeemed ranging from washing machine hose connections to car floor mats. The Warner was one of the first theaters in the country to do this. (Seaford's Palace held a similar event soon after.) A month later, the Warner was at it again with a scrap metal drive matinee for kids.

HISTORIC MOVIE THEATERS OF DELAWARE

This May 1942 photo shows F. Speer of the VFW presenting a check for $2,000 worth of war bonds to Donald Ross. The theater is not identified, but based on the date and the outside lettering just visible through the left exit, I believe this to be the Loew's Aldine. *Delaware Public Archives, Dover, Delaware.*

Collecting scrap wasn't theaters' only war effort. The Milton was a drop-off point for old phonograph records that would be collected and sent to troops; it also sold bonds and stamps commemorating the one-year anniversary of Pearl Harbor. Joining in the sale of bonds and stamps throughout the year were the Waller, the Everett, the Newark and the other Warner theaters in Wilmington. The Playhouse was the setting for a Red Cross conference, and even the Grand, which had temporarily closed in March 1942 for remodeling, contributed to the effort by lending its ticket booth for use as a bond and stamp sales point.

At the south end of the state, the Delmar Theatre screened *The Bugle Sounds* to raise funds for Delmar's new Civilian Defense First Aid Station, while up north, Claymont's Pike Theatre screened for air raid wardens the short government documentary *Fighting the Fire Bomb*. In between, the Ace Theatre in Wilmington's Polish community screened *This Is the Enemy*, a collection of short Russian propaganda films showing the ills of the Nazis.

The screening was preceded by a speech from municipal court judge Henry R. Isaacs, urging support of our ally Russia. (Earlier in the year, the Ace screened the first Soviet film about World War II, *Girl from Leningrad*.)

Managers of Wilmington theaters were required to take twenty hours of first aid training, plus ten hours of training for defense against chemical warfare. What they weren't trained to do was accompany movie star Paulette Goddard from Wilmington to Dover for a fundraising luncheon, which was followed by many appearances around the state, and ended with dinner at the Hotel du Pont. (Goddard had replaced Rita Hayworth in a late roster change.) She was accompanied by Warner manager Lewis Black, who, while not formally trained, rose to the task.

War efforts continued to dominate in 1943. Milford's New Plaza Theatre switched from fuel heat to coal as part of a conservation effort. Smyrna's Roxy helped raise money for the Red Cross. At military post theaters, WACs assumed operational responsibilities, while the Blue Hen, Loew's Aldine and newly built Ayers theaters were used as WAC recruiting stations. The Ritz,

In September 1942, as part of a war bond drive, movie star Paulette Goddard (*center*) paid a visit to many points in Delaware, including a luncheon in Dover. The woman holding Goddard's hand in the photo is Muriel Schwartz. *Delaware Public Archives, Dover, Delaware.*

the Waller and the Warner all held copper drives, with free screenings for thanks. The Warner also led the way in bond sales again, with many other theaters following suit, including the Blue Hen and the Lewes Auditorium. At the Pike, a war bond was a prize to one lucky theatergoer.

And at New Castle's Earle, a unique drive was organized by the local chapter of American Women's Voluntary Services: a junk jewelry drive. Unlike most other items collected to be reconstituted for use in warfare, junk jewelry was to be sent to troops in the Pacific to be used for barter. Nearly 1,800 pieces were collected.

In other war effort areas, the Warner was firing on all cylinders. The theater played host to film star Gene Lockhart, in town with fellow star Gail Patrick (who appeared at Loew's Aldine), to help raise money for the Red Cross; the Warner was a drop-off spot for vinyl phonograph donations (as was the Loew's Aldine and the National). The Warner also hosted a gala premiere of *This Is the Army*, which was preceded by a live show that included song-and-dance talent stationed at Forts DuPont and Miles, as well as a performance by the Jive Bombers of the New Castle Army Air Base. That event raised funds for Army Emergency Relief. The Warner was also considerate of details. Because of the shift work needed at defense plants, the theater experimented with opening earlier so workers could see a picture before their shift. This occurred when *Casablanca* opened at the theater in what appears to be the state premiere of the now-classic film.

But the biggest story within the biggest story is the cooperation among seventeen theaters around the state to premiere a slate of movies on June 21, 1944, all in the name of war bond sales.

For America's Fifth War Loan Drive, a collection of theater managers met in the office of Milford's mayor to discuss the plan. According to news reports, this was the only event of its kind in the country. Sales of war bonds to gain entrance to one of these premieres began on June 12 (a short window of time for such a massive event). Bonds were available for purchase at their respective theaters, with the exception of the Warner, whose bonds were available at all Wilmington theaters, plus at banks and other agencies licensed to sell bonds.

The theaters involved in the screenings (and their films, where available) were:

- Ayers Theatre (*Higher and Higher*)
- Ball Theatre
- Blue Hen Theatre

- Capitol Theatre (*Pin-Up Girl*)
- Diamond Theatre
- Earle Theatre (*Lady in the Dark*)
- Layton Theatre (*Rookies in Burma*)
- Lewes Auditorium (*Meet the People*)
- Milton Theatre
- National Theatre (*The Fighting Seabees*)
- New Plaza Theatre
- State Theatre (*Lady in the Dark*)
- Strand Theatre
- Waller Theatre
- Warner Theatre (*Up in Arms*)

(For reasons unreported, two theaters were slotted for June 25: the Crest with *What a Woman* and the Pike with *Hi Diddle Diddle*).

In 1944, the Warner Theatre (Wilmington) and sixteen other theaters around the state participated in the only war bond screening event of its kind in the country. Admission was exclusively an advance purchase of war bonds. Most theaters, like the Warner, held their events on June 21. *Delaware Public Archives, Dover, Delaware.*

And of course, it wouldn't be an event without a few stars in the Wilmington skies. Part of a parade and rally at Rodney Square in support of the loan drive included celebrities Mischa Auer, Rosemary Lane, John Payne, Dennis O'Keefe and William Holden. Early projections after the screenings were around $2 million raised. This would go toward the state's overall goal of $54 million for the Fifth War Loan Drive.

Yet for as sweeping a story as the bond drive of 1944 was, an amazing personal tale came out of the Warner in February 1945. Jeanne Peters of Richardson Park was one of countless war wives who wondered daily about the fate of her enlisted husband. With every (frequent) visit to the Warner, she watched newsreels with keen attention in hopes of seeing the love of her life and the father of their baby. One day, she thought she saw him onscreen. She sat through the same picture three times to be triply sure, then returned the next day with a friend to confirm it. Indeed, there was Corporal Theire J. Peters, part of a tank destroyer battalion in Luxembourg, on the big screen. Warner manager Lewis Black gave Mrs. Peters a strip of the film containing her husband's picture.

CLOSING CREDITS

1907–1941: Keller's Theatre

One night in March 1941, with about ten minutes of film remaining to play and only twenty-five patrons in the theater, the film reel in Keller's projection booth snapped and flared, starting a fire. The patrons left unscathed, but the projectionist suffered burns on his face and hands as he tried to control the blaze. About ninety minutes and four fire companies later, Keller's was a loss.

1923–1944: Ringler's Theatre

In September 1944, a hurricane hit Delaware, killing eleven. High winds and rough seas took considerable toll on the beach resorts. In Bethany, the entire boardwalk was leveled, including Ringler's. For all the closures of all the theaters in all the years, Ringler's appears to be the only theater to perish by natural disaster.

Historic Movie Theaters of Delaware

1916–1945: The Theater at Fort DuPont

Throughout the 1940s, the theater at Fort DuPont continued serving the military and the community, but not without challenges. In early 1940, the number of screenings was reduced due to the low number of personnel on base. And in 1941, civilians were barred from the theater beginning in September "in compliance with War Department orders." This is peculiar, considering the theater and the base had a history of encouraging civilian attendance and the order came just three months before the attack on Pearl Harbor. The theater closed in 1945, but the building still stands today, as if forgotten by time.

This is the theater at Fort DuPont as it appears today. To the left of the box office is a safe that was not part of the original theater. *Photo by Victoria Nazarewycz; photo produced with permission of Fort DuPont Redevelopment and Preservation Corp.*

FADE OUT

By the end of 1943, Delaware reached about the halfway point of its 150-year theatrical timeline, with approximately one hundred theaters having existed in the state. From that group, seven of the ten oldest were still in business. At the end of 1943, there were approximately forty-seven theaters open—almost half of all that had existed.

But that was then, and the state's landscape from that point forward would slowly shrink. Yes, Delaware would enjoy a slight spike in theater-count with the ongoing drive-in boom, but in the second seventy-five years of the state's history, only eight years would see forty-seven theaters or more, and no year would see that number after 1956.

LOST AND FOUND

Lost theater memories can be found around the state if you know where to look.

This row of vertical drawers is still in the projection booth at the theater at Fort DuPont. When the theater was in operation, they were used to hold film reels. *Photo by Victoria Nazarewycz; photo produced with permission of Fort DuPont Redevelopment and Preservation Corp.*

The projector at left is found in the projection booth at the theater at Fort DuPont, where it stood when it was originally used. Stripped of many parts, it is a haunting reminder of a long-gone era. *Photo by Victoria Nazarewycz; photo produced with permission of Fort DuPont Redevelopment and Preservation Corp.*

The photo below was taken from the stage, looking out into the theater at Fort DuPont, in 2017. There is a lot of disrepair, but each of the original four hundred seats is still bolted to the floor. *Photo by Victoria Nazarewycz; photo produced with permission of Fort DuPont Redevelopment and Preservation Corp.*

TAKE 8
THE 1950s

(Close) Out with the Old, (Drive) In with the New

FADE IN

"Out with the old, in with the new" really was the theme of the 1950s Delaware theater scene. On the "new" front, Delaware had drive-in fever. Riding the postwar wave started by the Brandywine and the Diamond State, all six of Delaware's confirmed public theaters to open in the 1950s were drive-ins, in places ranging from Wilmington to Delmar (for that town's second go at an open-air theater).

On the "old" front, three more of the state's first ten theatrical entities finally met their permanent fate, leaving only Middletown's Everett (oldest), Dover's Capitol (third oldest) and Wilmington's Grand (fourth oldest) to carry on the tradition of that exclusive club. Eleven old theaters in total would close in the decade. Blue-like laws continued to evolve at the local level, lawsuits would begin and end and desegregation would become a force.

OPENING CREDITS

Delmar Drive-In (2) | 1950–circa 1985
(Delmar)

After having its launch delayed a week because rain prevented the laying of asphalt, the Delmar Drive-In (2), with room for one thousand cars, opened on Friday, April 8, with the western romance *Relentless*. Two days later, police turned hundreds of cars away. Because of the way Delmar law was written, and because of where the theater was physically situated, blue laws still applied to the theater, making movies illegal at the Delmar on Sundays.

This would take months to resolve. First, a special referendum was held to include the land within town limits. That passed. But after one Sunday show in July, deputy attorney general Daniel Layton deemed the referendum itself unlawful, citing the referendum type needed to be part of a regular town election, not a special election. With the referendum unlawful, Sunday screenings were still illegal. Under advice of counsel stating the referendum was indeed valid, theater manager Nat Rosen showed a movie the following Sunday anyway. He was promptly arrested. For the next three Sundays, the show went on at the theater, and for the next three Sundays, whoever was managing the theater was promptly arrested (and posted bail and was back at work before the end credits rolled).

Little else is reported about the issue. Only an August 1950 news item cutely wondered who would be the fifth person arrested the following Sunday. In that article, though, the orders for the arrests were deemed a

This exterior photo of the DelMar Drive-In (2) is undated. The second open-air theater in the town's history was open from 1950 to 1984. *Delaware Public Archives, Dover, Delaware.*

mystery. Layton claimed he didn't order the arrests—he simply informed the police the screenings were illegal; no one knew where the arrest orders came from. The issue appears to have been resolved by the end of the season, as a later item mentions the theater closed out its year on Sunday, November 19. Other than having ninety speakers stolen in 1953, the rest of the decade was a quiet one for the Delmar.

Pleasant Hill Drive-In | 1950–circa 1984
(Newport)

Five months after the Delmar (2) opened, the Pleasant Hill Drive-In opened in Newport. The theater, with a capacity for about eight hundred cars, touted in its grand opening ad the things you would expect a drive-in to tout in its grand opening ad: no standing in line, no need for babysitters (kids under twelve free!), come as you are and so on. One unique perk the theater offered was a baby bottle–warming service. On opening night, the theater screened newsreels, shorts and *A Ticket to Mohawk*.

Kerry Drive-In | 1951–1961
(Wilmington)

Wilmington's first drive-in was the Kerry, located at Twenty-Eighth Street and Governor Printz Boulevard. The theater, with room for about 525 cars, also boasted a line of sight to the screen from the snack bar (as well as three different exit points to help disperse traffic). Owned by Bob Carpenter and named after the family dog, the Kerry was built on land that had previously been used by the Ringling Bros. Circus, leaving the displaced circus with only days to find a new home (it did). On opening night, the theater played newsreels, a Pete Smith Specialty short and *King Solomon's Mines*. In its second season, the theater became more family-focused with its film offerings, and in 1953, it also had speakers stolen—eighty-nine to be exact. Two years later, the theater shifted from being open during seasonal months to offering year-round screenings.

DelAir Drive-In/Dagsboro Drive-In | 1953–circa 1964
(Dagsboro)

Dagsboro, not content with just the Clayton, found itself caught up in the open-air fervor when the DelAir Drive-In debuted in 1953. There is one news item, in two separate sources, about the theater's owner being arrested for showing a burlesque picture in 1954, something considered at the time to be indecent. In both articles, the theater is referred to as the Dagsboro Drive-In. Given I found no other theatrical information with that specific name (but found DelAir references post-1954), I'm inclined to believe the use of "Dagsboro" in reporting the theater name is another case of a theater being associated with its town (like some opera houses were).

Midway Drive-In | 1953–circa 1982
(Rehoboth Beach)

The beach got in on the drive-in act in 1953 when William Derrickson opened the Midway in June on the Lewes-Rehoboth Highway. The drive-in had room for up to four hundred cars, but it also offered what was called an "open air auditorium" for those who wanted to view the film outside of an automobile. The first film screened was *All Ashore*. Heaters would be offered as part of the speaker equipment so the theater could remain open year-round. It moved to weekends-only in 1956.

Kent Drive-In | 1953–circa 1986
(Dover)

It didn't take long for the state capital to join in the open-air fun when the Kent Drive-In opened on South DuPont Highway in June. Opening information was not found, but on its first anniversary, the price of admission was one cent and it offered a Disney cartoon plus a double feature: *Small Town Girl* and *Northwest Stampede*. The Kent would be the last theater to open in the decade.

MOVING PICTURES

There was a strong community focus in 1950. In Bridgeville, the Sidney Theatre showcased photos of residents' children on the big screen in their "Hollywood Kiddie Parade." Up north, countless Wilmingtonians were soon-to-be-seen on the big screen, as cameras captured everyday life in the city for a documentary titled *Wilmington, 1950*; the film would later be shown at the Warner. Also at the Warner, the Huber Baking Company purchased one thousand tickets for underprivileged children to see *Cinderella*. Grown-ups got a treat, too, when stars Gale Storm and Dan Duryea appeared in person at the Queen to promote their new film, *The Underworld Story*.

Also that year was the death of the Savoy and the birth of the Towne in its place. Warner, the Savoy's owner, decided a complete replacement of the second-oldest theater in Wilmington (in existence at the time) was needed. After the last show on April 2, the Savoy was closed and demolition plans kicked off. A contest was held to rename the theater, and on December 1, the state-of-the-art Towne Theatre opened with Warner's *The Flame and the Arrow*.

Elsewhere in the early part of the decade, the Park Theatre struggled with low attendance, and after being unsuccessful in limiting its schedule, it closed in 1952, only to reopen under new management in 1954. Also in 1954, all theaters said bye-bye to blue laws as the state approved an updated bill that made legal the screening of films on Sundays, regardless of a town's incorporation status.

The year prior, in August 1953, the Warner installed a panoramic screen to be able to present "for the first time" (a claim with no caveats) a 3-D film: *Second Chance* starring Robert Mitchum (who once lived in Felton). But for all of the Warner's might, installing a new screen was child's play compared to what happened at the Reese. Seven months prior to the Warner's upgrade, Reese Harrington signed a contract to install in his theater the new RCA Syncro-Screen to show 3-D films using "Cycglorama," a method employed to add depth to moving images (in concert with the viewer wearing red- and green-lensed glasses). The first film shown at the Reese (and, most likely, the first film shown in Delaware) using this technology was the western *Hiawatha*, the presentation of which was met with rave reviews (at least according to the theater). Shortly after, the Reese screened the first truly 3-D film, *Bwana Devil*. In with the new, indeed.

The next year, Reese Harrington continued to dominate the scene, this time with more than fancy tech tricks. It began in May 1954, when he hosted what could easily be called an entertainment summit, inviting community members from sixteen nearby towns to join him in a roundtable discussion about how his theater could improve its projection, sound, screen size, general presentation and even decorations and other creature comforts. The group was dubbed the Central Committee of the Community of Friendly Neighbors. (Okay. They could have use a little help branding.)

In response to what he took away from the summit, Harrington committed to upgrading his sound system, closing the theater each Wednesday until complete. Also on Wednesdays, Harrington had installed what was believed to be the largest screen in lower Delaware: the Giant Magda, which was unanimously selected by the committee. The screen used something called the "under-up illusion of reflected light," which purportedly eliminated eye strain, while the "Reflecto Process" made images onscreen appear more real. In July, the theater adopted the Movie-Rama system, which altered sight lines and leveraged the Magda to make the audience feel like they were part of each film. Finally, in September, Harrington unveiled the whole lot (including 4-Track Stereophonic sound) to present *Gone with the Wind*.

A large group stands outside the Milton Theatre one night in June 1956 as police officer William "Bill" Betts stands guard. Going on inside the theater (or having recently ended) is an anti–school integration meeting. *Courtesy of the Lydia Black Cannon Museum & Milton Historical Society, Milton, Delaware.*

HISTORIC MOVIE THEATERS OF DELAWARE

The picture on the left was taken around 1899, when the building was known as the Clayton House. The picture on the right was taken about 1958, when it was known by the name it's known by today: The Queen. *Delaware Public Archives, Dover, Delaware.*

One of the greatest stars in Hollywood history dropped in on Wilmington in 1955. Cary Grant, traveling to Philadelphia for the opening of *To Catch a Thief*, was guest of honor at a cocktail party and dinner at the Hotel du Pont (courtesy of, among others, the Warner theaters). While in town, Grant revisited the Playhouse, where he had appeared on stage years before as a child actor.

Also in 1955, the Brandywine Drive-In was sold and renamed the Ellis Drive-In. In 1956, with all resort area theaters struggling for business, the Lewes Auditorium and Blue Hen Theatre closed. In 1957, the Warner fell victim to a considerable fire. It was fully repaired and remodeled, and in April, it reopened with *Cinderella*. And two years later, in April 1959, the Queen closed its doors after a screening of *The House on Haunted Hill*.

Two major stories came out of the 1950s—one with cultural significance and one with social significance.

While the story of cultural significance has its roots prior to the 1950s, it took flight in this decade as Hollywood continued to push the morality envelope and theaters joined them. Still, there was room for protest. Elia Kazan's *Baby Doll* was set to be screened at the Warner in early 1957. The film doesn't hide its sexuality, which drew protests from area students at four Catholic high schools, the Knights of Columbus and the women of the Sodality of the Blessed Virgin Mary of St. Peter's Cathedral. The Warner delayed the open of the picture by one week, but ultimately the show went on.

On the heels of those protests, 1958 saw a controversy surrounding another film, this being screened at the Edge Moor Theatre: Roger

Vadim's *And God Created Woman*. The film is about an eighteen-year-old nymphet (Brigitte Bardot) and the three men who get worked into a lather over her. The film opened at the Edge Moor on February 12. In the audience that night was Attorney General Joseph Craven, his deputy and a state trooper. After seeing the film, Craven wanted the screenings stopped because he believed the film was "offensive to the common sense of decency and modesty of the community."

In the wake of that first Wilmington screening, the attorney general directed police to halt all future screenings and arrest anyone associated if screenings were attempted. After legal action taken by theater proprietor Daniel Cudone, a restraining order was issued against the attorney general, prohibiting the stoppage of the film, as well as prohibiting the arrest of any theater employees for screening the film (but still allowing for Cudone to be arrested).

Meanwhile, the demand to see the film gave the Edge Moor two things every theater wants: sellouts of current shows and lines waiting for future shows. In fact, Cudone expanded screenings to three per weekday and five on Sunday (take that, defunct blue laws). Also, some local clergy came to Cudone's defense, citing civil liberties outweighed film content. The attorney general ultimately took no further action, and because of that, the court dismissed the restraining order and the issue quietly went away. (All of this happened in the wake of another story about screenings and morality, the details of which can be found in the Manor Theatre's Closing Credits.)

But the big story of the decade—really the one with the greatest societal impact in the history of Delaware theaters—began in 1951 when Wilmington theaters started admitting people of color on the same basis as white people. In advance of several civil rights bills expected to be introduced in the general assembly, six city theaters announced they would begin admitting people of color: the Warner, Loew's Aldine, Towne, Grand, Queen and Arcadia. According to reports, the Ace and Rialto planned to continue to exercise their rights to refuse service to people of color. Rialto manager AJ Belair was even quoted as saying, "I'm not admitting Negroes and I never will. I would close the theater before I'd let them in. Let them go to their own theater."

A storm was coming to the city.

Along the same theme, but south of the city and later in the decade (1956), the NAACP planned a boycott of six theaters. According to reports, it was "the first organized economic boycott to be announced in Delaware in connection with the integration/segregation dispute." Five of the theaters were owned by the Schwartz family: the Everett, Smyrna, Temple and Capitol, plus the Kent Drive-In. The sixth theater named was the independently owned Diamond State Drive-In in Felton.

The complaint was that people of color were forbidden from sitting on the main floor and relegated to the theaters' balconies. (White people were allowed to sit wherever they wanted, including the balcony.) In the case of the Temple, the balcony was purported to have only benches, not seats. At the two drive-ins, it was alleged people of color were segregated to park in a specific area. Muriel Schwartz denied the drive-in allegation for her theater and the NAACP later confirmed segregation was not practiced there, but that theater was included in the boycott because it was part of the Schwartz chain.

Prior to the boycott, which began organically and was later organized by the NAACP, Dr. George Kent of Delaware State University had requested several meetings with Schwartz to discuss desegregation in her theaters, but no meeting was ever scheduled. Schwartz's position, regardless of the boycott, was that her theaters "would follow the customs of the community as we have in the past. We alone cannot take a stand on the matter."

CLOSING CREDITS

1920–circa 1952: Green Lantern Theatre | Don Theatre | Pike Theatre

The Pike wasn't long for the 1950s. In the first year of the decade, the theater made a little news with a very public boycott of road work being done on Philadelphia Pike, and in 1951, it hosted a benefit where admission was *a pack of cigarettes to be donated to a hospital*. The theater closed sometime between Christmas 1951 and the spring of 1953, when it was purchased by the Bible Baptist Church.

1920–1952: The Strand

The Strand's closure wasn't avoided for lack of trying. It went through management changes and closures/reopens in 1950 and 1951, and it tried shifting its screening focus to foreign films in an attempt to cater to a different audience. It even went so far as to remove the popcorn machine (citing complaints of the smell), jettisoning newsreels ("full of war and grief") and setting firm policies on the presence of children. None of that worked, and by 1952 the whole thing was closed and for sale.

1879–circa 1954: New Castle Opera House

Coverage of the closing of the state's fifth-oldest theater is sparse. The last historical news mention comes in 1954 when a *Morning News* column references a live show happening on the "rather shabby setting of the [NCOH's] antiquated second floor."

1915–circa 1954: Elcora Theatre | Delmar Theatre | Avenue Theatre

In its final years, the Avenue found itself as part of a lawsuit filed against its owners by seven different film studios. The accusation was falsifying ticket sales data in the interest of keeping film rental costs down. It closed around 1954, but in grand Delaware theater tradition, it suffered from a fire in 1956.

Circa 1884–circa 1955: Armory Hall | Shore Theatre

The Shore Theatre went out with a whimper. The last film listing I found was in 1950, and the last use for something entertainment-related was a vaudeville show in 1955. As for the antitrust lawsuit it filed against Schine, including what had become the Plaza Theatre, plus all those Hollywood studios, that case was dismissed "on the stipulation of the parties involved."

Circa 1880–circa 1956: The Auditorium

Coverage of the Auditorium appears to have been nonexistent, but a piece in a later edition of the *Morning News* cites there were seventy-seven years of activity at the Auditorium, putting its approximate closure year at 1956.

1917–circa 1956: Temple Theatre

There's a theme here in the 1950s where theater closings weren't as newsworthy as they once had been, and the Temple Theatre appears to be no different. The last news item for the theater was that it was one of the theaters named in the 1956 NAACP boycott.

1921–1956: The Arcadia

In 1951, Warner was required to sell the Arcadia as a result of a government ruling that limited the number of theaters a movie studio could own in a given city. In 1953, 3-D equipment was installed, and the first 3-D film to screen there was the western *The Stranger Wore a Gun*. Not being a first-run house, and unable to compete with drive-ins for second-run films, the theater closed in May 1956 after the double feature of *Rock around the Clock* and *Fury at Gunsight Pass*.

1949–1957: Manor Theatre

Despite the statewide shift in attitudes toward the exhibition of films on Sundays, the content of films screened (any day of the week) still came under considerable scrutiny, criticism, complaint and, on occasion, legal decision. Such was the fate of the Manor Theatre in the first half of the century.

In late March/early April 1950, the Manor worked into its screening schedule some burlesque films, which caused community problems. The opening salvo was the Wilmington Manor Civic Association's formal protestation of burlesque film screenings there and the formation of a committee within the association to work with the theater to prevent future screenings. Apparently that didn't work.

In January 1951, the Manor screened a burlesque picture titled *Hollywood Peep Show* (a.k.a. *Everybody's Girl*). Directed by Lillian Hunt, the film is a live burlesque show performed onstage in front of what seems to be a very small audience (or perhaps only the film crew), and it contains what one would expect from a burlesque show: live music, comedy sketches and a parade of shapely women, performing solo or in groups, stripping out of numerous costumes. Although there is no frontal nudity, creative costuming regularly gives that impression. It is tame by today's standards (and I found the film to be incredibly dull by any standard) but at the time it was racy, and the New Castle community to which the theater was home wanted no parts of racy. (It also wanted no parts of the parking problems created in front of businesses and homes near the theater, caused by the many out-of-state theatergoers coming to see burlesque pictures.)

Formal complaints were filed, and newly minted attorney general H. Albert Young dispatched state police to the theater, where they arrested manager John Scope and projectionist Charles Emerson. Less than a week later, the men were charged with "exhibiting and showing an obscene, lewd, lascivious, filthy, and indecent film, figure or image, to wit, a motion picture entitled 'Hollywood Peep Show.'" Scope was also charged with possession with intent to exhibit, posting film-related pictures on the outer and inner walls of the theater and advertising the film in local papers. The theater was allowed to remain in operation during all of this.

The March trial eventually found the entire courtroom—presiding judges, jury (nine men/three women), attorney general staff, defendants, attorneys and witnesses—at the Crest Theatre to watch the film. The attorney general said he would prove the film (and the advertising) was "offensive to the sense of decency and modesty, and calculated to arouse sensual passion and sexual emotions in those who witness it." Despite the defense attorney's claims of censorship, it took the jury two hours to return their verdict. Scope was found guilty of all eight counts against him; projectionist Emerson was acquitted entirely. Scope's attorney's request for a retrial was denied, and Scope's final penalty, some fifteen months after his arrest, was a $250 fine (for the exhibition counts) and one year's probation (for the other charges).

On Valentine's Day 1954, John Scope died of a heart attack at age forty-one. The theater operated until 1957.

1916–1958: National Theatre | Hopkins Theatre

The National enjoyed a fine run serving Wilmington's black community, and while it may have been a sad day when it closed in 1951, sorrow was replaced with joy when the Hopkins Theatre, owned by the same family, opened almost next door to take its place the next day (thus continuing the single theatrical entity). As the sole theater in the city to cater to people of color, the Hopkins opened to a sellout crowd of 750, with Mayor James Hearn in attendance. The film shown was *Vengeance Valley*. In 1956, owner John O. Hopkins, former sixteen-term member of city council, passed away at age sixty-six. At his viewing, former governor Walter Bacon and former heavyweight champion Joe Louis paid their respects. The theater would close two years later, in part due to a decline in business as a result of theater integration, which gave the Hopkins's core customer base more choices around the city.

1904–circa 1958: Newark Theatre

The Newark Theatre received little fanfare over the course of its existence, including its closure. The last news item I found was in 1958 for a children's event at Christmas hosted by the local Chrysler plant.

SEEKING STARDOM

Super 113 Drive-In | circa 1953–circa 1964
(Milford)

According to DriveIns.org, the Super 113 opened at 802 North DuPont Boulevard in Milford in 1953, had space for about four hundred cars and closed in 1964. I found only two news items about the theater, both from 1955. One was a listing as part of a larger ad in the *Philadelphia Inquirer* for the screening of *Sins of Pompeii*. The other was an item in an October edition of the *Morning News* in which Cub Scouts were planning to see a double feature at the theater.

Shalimar Theatre | 1959–2006
(Middletown)

Of all the theaters in this book, the Shalimar might be the most obscure and the most magical.

Gordon Brinckle hailed from Philadelphia and spent his life obsessed with movie theaters. He apprenticed as a theater decorator, but he excelled at general design and architecture. Over the coming years, he took jobs in Philadelphia theaters to stay close to his love, finding a passion for projection work. It was too difficult to break into the projectionists' union, but when he was drafted into World War II, Brinckle listed his profession as projectionist, which led to him screening military training films and Hollywood pictures at bases around the United States and Asia. When he returned home, he was hired by the Everett, first as a doorman, then manager and then projectionist, a title he held until the theater (temporarily) closed in 1979.

But in 1959, he took it upon himself to build in the basement of his Middletown home the Shalimar Theatre—a fully functional nine-seat theater, complete with a sixteen-millimeter projector, a screen with a curtain, footlights, nineteen speakers hidden in the ceiling and walls to fill the room with sound from the working organ, a marquee and an aesthetic that harkened back to the movie palaces of the 1930s.

Over the years, this Renaissance man constantly tinkered with the place, but he never regularly entertained people there. For him, the Shalimar was the realization of his lifelong dream to own a movie palace, as well as an effort to preserve the history of the movie palaces of old. Brinckle died in 2007, but

Above: The Shalimar: Delaware's Last Movie Palace. *Photo by and courtesy of Kendall Messick.*

Opposite: Shalimar projection booth. *Photo by and courtesy of Kendall Messick.*

the year before, he had expressed concerns to historian and author Kendall Messick, who had been documenting Brinckle's life, that the Shalimar would be demolished upon his death. Messick suggested deconstructing the theater and reassembling it as part of a traveling exhibit for Messick's book (and subsequent documentary). That vision was realized as well.

While the Shalimar wasn't a traditional theater, I wanted to include it here because of its uniqueness as a full-blown "home theater" in an era when such a thing didn't exist as it does today, but more so because the Shalimar epitomized the magic of movie theaters in a way titans like the Everett, Grand or Warner never could.

FADE OUT

With changes in everything from how films were exhibited to who could see what films, where and when, the 1950s, regardless of net open/close numbers, represented a time of incredible change. That the last new theater to open in the decade was in 1953 seems to speak not about the interest in growth but about how the changes to the existing landscape were as important as expanding that landscape.

LOST AND FOUND

Lost theater memories can be found around the state if you know where to look.

This original drive-in speaker (*below, top*) once hung from car windows at the Diamond State Drive-In, long before they went to wireless FM. This artifact is on display at the Felton Museum. *Photo by Victoria Nazarewycz.*

These undated, original, unused tickets (*below, bottom*) from the Lewes Auditorium are now part of the Lewes Historical Society archives. *Lewes Historical Society.*

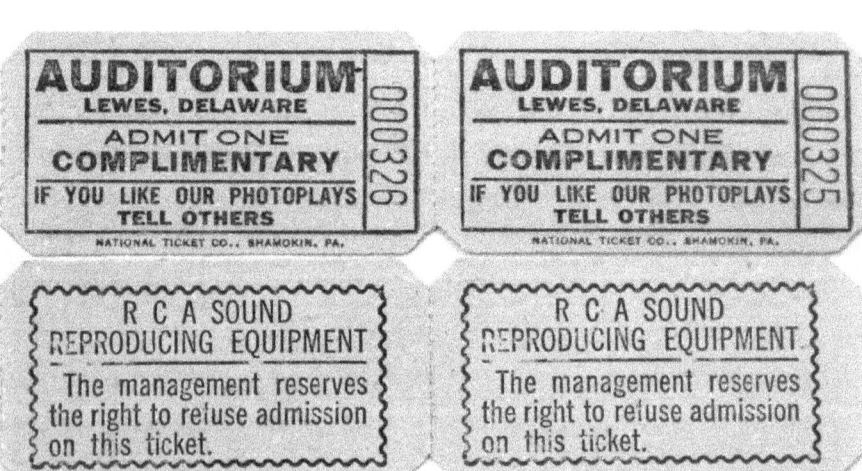

TAKE 9
THE 1960s

Equality for All, Immorality for Some

FADE IN

The drive-in craze wasn't over yet in Delaware in the 1960s, but it wasn't impervious, either. Three new open-air theaters opened in the state (the last of the state's new drive-ins to open), but two closed. Among all theaters, numbers continued to dwindle. Although a total of eight new theaters opened in the decade, fourteen theaters closed for good, and another four went dark temporarily.

The theme of moviegoing in the 1960s didn't find its groove until late, as many theaters, facing tough competition from one another and other forms of entertainment, shifted exhibition focus from first- or second-run fare to cheaper-to-acquire grindhouse and exploitation films. When the MPAA ratings system was born in 1968, so too was the X-rating. Films given this rating—either by the MPAA or by the filmmakers (which was perfectly legal)—were embraced by theaters as screening alternatives with a growing popularity.

OPENING CREDITS

Prices Corner Drive-In | 1962–1979
(Wilmington)

Almost ten years had passed since the last new theater in the state had opened and even more time than that since the first new theater in Wilmington. The one-thousand-car Price's Corner Drive-In opened on April 6 with a double-feature: *Blue Hawaii* and *The Comancheros*. In addition to enticing parents by offering free admission to children under twelve, the theater also offered free milk for baby bottles (and free bottle-warming). At the end of the decade, the theater made the foray into mature fare with a film titled *Sweden: Heaven and Hell*. Called a "disgusting documentary" about Sweden by the *News Journal*, the Italian-made film featured a series of sexually charged sequences, although apparently with little actual nudity.

Cinema Center | 1963–2015*
Main Street Movies 5 | 2017–present
(Newark)

With the opening of Cinema Center in Newark in October 1963, Delaware had its first new indoor movie theater since the Manor opened in 1949. Built in the Newark Shopping Center, the six-hundred-seater was the latest theater in the Schwartz circuit, which was slowly expanding north. It was also the first theater in Delaware built in a shopping center, a trend that would continue. The theater offered three rows of seating equipped with devices for the hearing impaired, a room on the second floor for private parties and a free coffee bar. The Cinema Center seemed interested in attracting a different crowd. Its opening picture wasn't a flashy release or the latest Disney film but rather a French comedy, *The Suitor*. Early in its history, the theater also housed the Cinema Center Art Gallery, where artistic works such as paintings and drawings were put on display.

The Cinema Center in Newark opened in 1963 and featured art exhibits as part of its attraction. This photo is undated, but the *Goldfinger* poster on the left suggests 1964. *Delaware Public Archives, Dover, Delaware.*

Cinema 141 | 1964–1988
AMC Cinema 141 | 1988–1993
Cinema 141 | 1993–1998
(Wilmington)

In what was believed to have been the first indoor/outdoor theater pairing in the east, the one-thousand-seat Cinema 141 was built adjacent to the Prices Corner Drive-In and opened in June with the Delaware premiere of *The World of Henry Orient*. The opening-night festivities included a parade, search lights, a live band and an appearance by Miss Delaware 1964. Over the decade, Cinema 141 offered tickets by mail to select screenings, a practice that grew in popularity around the state, whether for long-running hits like *The Sound of Music* (in its twenty-third week of engagement) or premieres like *Doctor Dolittle* and *The Lion in Winter*. An early X-rater for the theater was *De Sade*, a bio-drama starring Keir Dullea, who is probably best known for playing Dave in *2001: A Space Odyssey*.

Midway Palace | 1965–1998
Movies at Midway | 1999-Present
(Rehoboth Beach)

In 1954, the year after William Derrickson built the Midway Drive-In, he developed the Midway Shopping Center. Eleven years later, William's son Richard opened his first theater in that shopping center: the single-screen, 850-seat Midway Palace. The first movie shown there was *Mister Moses*.

Naamans Drive-In | 1968–1987
(Claymont)

When the Naamans Drive-In opened in May 1968, its owner boasted it would be the first drive-in theater in the country with air conditioning. Really. In-car air conditioning units, developed by Budco Quality Theatres, were available to customers. Budco also claimed the units worked as heaters in the winter. While its opening film was the drama *The Sand Pebbles*, it wasn't long before the theater worked grittier B-movies into its rotation—a rotation it kept spry. For example, in November 1968, its programming changed from *The Parent Trap* and *Cool Hand Luke* one week to *Poor White Trash* and *Shanty Tramp* the next to *Thunderball* and *From Russia with Love* the following week. An early X-rater it showed was *Vixen!*, from director Russ Meyer.

Cinemart | 1968–1980
(Wilmington)

A month after Naamans opened came the one-thousand-seat Cinemart (often spelled CineMart or Cine'Mart), located opposite the Merchandise Mart on Governor Printz Boulevard. Its first true screening was an invitation-only benefit for the Brandywine Hundred Fire Company that included a pre-film cocktail party. The film selected, as well as the one played for the general public the next night, was Neil Simon's *The Odd Couple*.

HISTORIC MOVIE THEATERS OF DELAWARE

Dover Cinema | 1969–circa 1985*
Blue Hen Mall Theater | 1987–circa 1989
Blue Hen Mall Concert Hall | circa 1989–circa 1998
(Dover)

Prior to March 1969, the Capitol was the only public indoor theater open in Dover. That changed when the Dover Cinema opened in the Blue Hen Mall. Because of its location inside a mall (which appears to be the first instance of that in the state), parking was not an issue. Still, despite modern design and comforts, the theater decided its maiden screening would be 1939's *Gone with the Wind*.

The Dover Cinema was located inside the Blue Hen Mall. It was an early example of the mall/theater partnership that would flourish in Delaware in the 1970s and 1980s. The picture is undated, but the screening suggests it was taken opening weekend, 1969. *Delaware Public Archives, Dover, Delaware.*

Newark Drive-In | 1969–circa 1984
(Newark)

In terms of openings, the decade ended the way it began: with a new drive-in. It was based in Newark, a first for that town, joining the historic State and the recently opened Cinema Center. Its August 20 opening double feature was *The Bridge at Remagen* and *Ring of Bright Water*. The theater advertised the usual new drive-in features, like an air-conditioned snack bar and electric in-car heaters, but it also advertised having a covered patio, complete with tables and chairs, for those who didn't want to drive into the drive-in.

MOVING PICTURES

After some business was conducted in 1960—both the Delmar Drive-In (2) and the Milton Theatre were sold, the former to the Schwartz family—there was a flurry of activity around the state, mostly involving peculiar screenings and events, or peculiar closures and reopenings.

In 1960 Felton, the Diamond State Drive-In ran afoul of the law when it attempted to screen the nudist film *Nature's Paradise*. Police had other plans, so to the disappointment of the hundreds who came to see the film, the theater instead screened a double feature of *The Shameless Sex* and *Cover Girl Killer*. About half the cars stayed. In 1961, the Smyrna Theatre announced a four-opera series, with two screenings each of *Aida*, *Il Trovatore*, *Madame Butterfly* and *La Traviata*. Loew's Aldine was playing the mainstream *Ben Hur*, but during its run, manager Edgar J. Doob refused to sell popcorn, saying, "Popcorn and *Ben Hur* just don't go together."

In 1962, Mother Nature flooded the Broadkill River, which in turn flooded the Milton Theatre above the seats; the theater would (at least temporarily) persevere. In 1963, the City of Wilmington shut down the Ace due to fire doors being nailed shut, heating ducts being filled with trash and leaking water pouring onto electrical fixtures (to name just a few violations). New management, new improvements and new art house programming would breathe life into the old place with its new name, the Capri Art Theater. It would become the third theater in the city to specialize in art house films, the first being the Edge Moor, which had been programming such films for several years, and the second being the Towne, which had announced its programming shift a week prior.

In 1964, the Warner offered several closed-circuit telecasts of the Beatles, who were part of a larger rock show that included Leslie Gore and the Beach Boys. A year later, for a different audience, it screened the Clay-Patterson fight. Approximately 1,300 people filled the 1,700-seat theater for that. Also in 1964, the Lewes Auditorium, which had been dormant for about a decade, was sold and reopened as the Lewes Theater.

The Rehoboth landscape changed in early 1966 when the Blue Hen Theatre was one of three Rehoboth Avenue businesses destroyed by a raging blaze. (The clothing store where the fire began, as well as a gift shop, were the other two.) The theater rebuilt in time for the new summer season. It was named the Beachwood. And dealing with fire of a different kind was the Milton Theatre. Its scheduled screening of *The Klansmen* invited a threat by a supposed member of the KKK that the theater would find itself the

HISTORIC MOVIE THEATERS OF DELAWARE

Above: In addition to traditional popcorn and Coke, the long concession counter at the DelMar Drive-In (2) (1967) offered burgers, steak sandwiches, pizza and what appears to be orange drink. The cash register is just to the right of the candy rack. *Delaware Public Archives, Dover, Delaware.*

Right: In 1965, the Diamond State Drive-In planned its screenings at least a month in advance, as evidenced by this handy reminder from July—suitable for hanging! This artifact is on display at the Felton Museum. *Felton Museum.*

135

recipient of a burning cross if it screened the film. The show went on, but no cross burned. (I could find no film from that era called *The Klansmen*, but I did find a 1966 film called *The Black Klansmen*, a.k.a. *I Crossed the Color Line*, about a black man who poses as a white man to infiltrate the KKK after they kill his daughter.)

In 1967, a pair of Wilmington theater institutions saw somewhat temporary ends. The first, in February, was the Towne Theatre, Wilmington's oldest movie house. The building was sold, and the new owners had plans for a two-block enclosed shopping mall. The theater's lease, though, was valid until 1970; still, they decided to close early, and the last film was *La Dolce Vita*. But in one of the more peculiar moments I've seen, the theater reopened temporarily that summer for no other reason than to screen the first-run film *Hawaii*. On June 28, the theater reopened and played that film only, twice a day, every day, until October 5. Management indicated it would reopen the theater again if the right situation presented itself, but it wouldn't—at least not in the 1960s.

The second Wilmington institution was the Grand, which fell four years short of having entertained people for one hundred years. As the landscape changed in the city, as well as within the film exhibition business, Grand owner Stanley-Warner had no interest in renewing the lease on the theater. While it was once Wilmington's largest stage and an early pioneer in film exhibition, the Grand's film offerings over the years had slowly degraded until it was left with screening discarded pictures that had already run at drive-ins. On June 30, the Grand showed a double feature of *Hotel* and, fittingly, *The Game Is Over*. When the audience left, the lights went out and an era appeared to have ended. But in 1969, Chuck Powell of Minquadale single-handedly breathed life back into it. He purchased projection equipment from the Warner Company, signed a lease with the Masons and, on April 30, started showing movies there again. He opened with the Wilmington premiere of *Tarzan of the Great River*, followed by *The Brotherhood*. Powell wanted to bring families back to the movies and let kids in for fifty cents, just like the old days.

In 1968, at the Capri Art Theater, screenings were the target of protests. Reverend John Flinn, new associate pastor at St. Hedwig's Catholic Church, led picketers to rail against the "girlie movies" that were part of the theater's regular rotation (as it had expanded from art house films). Their signs, with slogans like *Blessed are the clean of heart* and *Clean it up or close it up*, were met with the theater's own signs, which had been taped to the box office window and included *Do as I want you to do or I'll picket your business* and *I pay taxes. Does the Church?* The Capri argued kids weren't admitted to those types of shows, while the protestors argued kids were still exposed to titles and

These two letters are an exchange between the Edge Moor Theatre and the Diocese of Wilmington. Ever polite, both organizations remained firm in their positions. Those "films shown there in the past" surely include *And God Created Woman*, the film that brought a lot of attention—good and bad—to the theater. *The Archives of the Catholic Diocese of Wilmington.*

posters. That same year, James Fred Evans, manager of the Milton Theatre, was arrested on an obscenities charge when he screened *Motel Confidential*, a cheapie sexploitation film. When he pleaded innocent several months later, his lawyer indicated the theater had since closed.

But all of this combined couldn't compare to *the* story of the 1960s—the one that took place at the Rialto, where the storm had begun brewing the decade before.

To recap, in the early 1950s, other city theaters adopted nondiscriminatory policies, but the Rialto stood in dissent, refusing to allow people of color into the theater. When the chairman of the State Human Relations Commission attempted to meet with the theater to discuss its position, the Rialto's response was, "If he wants to see us he can come down; we're not going up to see him." The Rialto was one of the few discriminatory holdouts among all Wilmington businesses (theaters or otherwise), but given the laws of the time, there was nothing the city, county or state could do.

In November 1962, a biracial community group that came to be known as Concerned Citizens picketed the Rialto with signs reading *Don't Support Segregation with Your Dollars, Discrimination Destroys Democracy* and *Education Says*

No to Segregation. In response, the theater doubled down, reiterating that the Human Relations Committee could come to them (not vice versa), adding, "This is our place of business. It is a private business and we have the right to deny admission to anyone we choose." The Rialto even argued theaters *without* segregation had had violent disturbances as a result.

When the committee requested a neutral meeting site, the theater declined, and when the committee finally acquiesced and went to the theater for the discussion, Rialto co-owner Harry Brubaker wouldn't even conduct the meeting in an office; instead, he carried on the discussion while taking tickets from patrons. Theater manager Richard Lewis was further quoted as saying, "We aren't going to submit no matter what happens. Even if they passed a law and told us to do otherwise, I think the owners would rather close the place down."

The picketing continued. Also vocal about the issue was Wilmington mayor John E. Babiarz, who went on record as saying he refused to patronize the Rialto because of the policy. Also in formal support of the protests were the Episcopal bishop of Delaware and the Wilmington district superintendent of the Methodist Church. At the end of 1962, picketing, which had been going on every weekend for over a month, was suspended for the holidays, both as an act of goodwill and as an opportunity for the State Human Relations Committee to again meet with Rialto management.

In early 1963, the movement for racial equality spread across the state. In Kent and Sussex Counties, there was steady, voluntary movement toward integration in all businesses, including Dover's Capitol Theatre, where people of color were no longer relegated to the balcony. In lower New Castle County, the Town of Middletown announced that "no one would be refused the privilege and rights of service and attendance," including at the Everett Theatre. But the focus was still on the Rialto. When talks stalled between the committee and the theater in early January, picketing resumed and was intended to last the month. By the end of January, though, the Concerned Citizens announced their protest would go on indefinitely. Tensions began to rise.

A group of African exchange students from Lincoln University in Oxford, Pennsylvania, attempted to purchase tickets at the Rialto one April night and were turned away at the exterior box office. To accommodate others in line behind the students, the theater created a makeshift ticket booth inside the lobby. Another patron said the students could go ahead in line, but once inside the theater, the students were accused of trespassing. All students were arrested but one, an American who had remained outside; he was charged with disorderly conduct. The African students planned to reach out to their respective embassies in Washington.

Ministers began to organize and urged their congregations to take action by contacting their government leaders to enact change. Students and faculty at Lincoln University were planning their own pickets. The local chapter of the NAACP warned of "impending civil rights unrest." By the end of the month, Governor Carvel publicly suggested perhaps legislation should be passed to address the issue regionally, beginning first with New Castle County.

Finally, on Wednesday, May 1, the Rialto, after remaining stubbornly adamant for six months, succumbed to social and political pressure and announced it was changing its policy immediately. Theater ownership explained they had remained so resolute because they thought that was what the majority of their customers wanted.

Okay. Got it.

In December 1963, by a vote of 10–7, the state senate passed HB 466, commonly known as the Public Accommodations Bill, giving equal access of most goods and services to the public, regardless of race. Governor Carvel signed the bill into law on December 18.

As something of a postscript, the passage of the Public Accommodations Bill didn't put a complete end to the black community's challenges. That year, Dr. Doris Mitchell, a woman of color, filed a formal complaint against the Clayton Theatre, stating she was asked to move from her first-floor seat to the balcony. The theater refuted that claim. Hers was one of the first six complaints filed across the state. Negotiations with the theater seemed hopeful at the time of the last news report.

CLOSING CREDITS

1942–1960: Crest Theatre

The Crest closed without warning or fanfare on October 15. Its last double feature was *Hell to Eternity* and *The Black Shield of Falworth*.

1921–circa 1961: New Theatre | Palace Theatre

Like the Crest, the Palace in Seaford closed with little fanfare. The last mention I found in news items was from 1961, when a protest rally *against* the Teamsters Union was scheduled to occur there.

1948–1961: Sidney Theatre

Many things can be attributed to the demise of theaters: poor management, competition, fire and so forth. But the reason for the Sidney closing, according to manager Ken Holson, is really something else. Per Holson, the decline in business at the Sidney, which appears to have led to its closure, was due to people having a greater interest in church and community. He believed the closing of the theater marked the end of the era when people looked for entertainment.

1951–1961: Kerry Drive-In

In the postwar era, the Kerry was the fifth of fourteen drive-ins to open but the first to close. In the summer of 1961, Wilmington City Council looked for property for a new municipal arena; the Kerry was on part of the property it looked at. In late November, the Kerry announced it was closing for the season after its screenings of *Ocean's 11* and *Jungle Attack* and would be back the following spring. It never returned. The land was sold.

1921–1962: Parkway Theatre | Adams' Parkway Theatre | Parkway Theatre | Loew's Theatre | Ritz Theatre

And here I thought the reason for the Sidney closing was unique. The Ritz closed, it seems, because of the creation of I-95, which cut through the heart of the city and along the corridor where the theater was located. Its final double feature was crooner-heavy: *The Joker Is Wild* starring Frank Sinatra and *Too Late the Blues* starring Bobby Darin.

1941–1962: Avenue Theatre

The headline of the December 17 *Morning News* said it all: "Fire Levels 4 Buildings in Rehoboth." One of those buildings was the Avenue. On December 16, at approximately 2:50 p.m., a fire broke out in the overheated chimney of the Avenue Restaurant. For four hours the fire raged, taking out the restaurant, the Candy Box candy store, the Avenue Jewelry Store, an apartment above those and the six-hundred-seat theater.

1942–1963: The Theater at Fort Miles

While it isn't clear exactly when the second on-base theater closed, according to the Fort Miles Historical Association, a theater existed at the base postwar, and the postwar base was used by the navy to listen for Russian submarines until 1963.

1953–circa 1964: DelAir Drive-In/Dagsboro Drive-In

The Dagsboro Drive-In was the next open-air theater in the postwar era to find itself out of business. I found nothing specific about its closure beyond the year cited by DriveIns.org.

1912–circa 1965: Peoples Theatre | Ryons Theatre | Sussex Theatre | Ayers Theatre

Short of a mention as being a possible subject of a 1964 complaint for violating the Public Accommodations Law (a complaint that does not look like it was filed), the Ayers Theatre went about its business in the 1960s, until, due to dwindling attendance, it folded around 1965.

Circa 1900–1966: Reese Opera House | Reese Theatre

Following the path of many historic theaters that closed in the 1960s, the Reese, despite its heralded commitment to community and technology in the 1950s, quietly ended its run in 1966.

1913–1967: Waller Theatre | New Waller Theatre

On the night of Saturday, July 10, 1967, about one hundred patrons were inside the Waller. One child yelled when he noticed a crack opening in the ceiling. Patrons escaped unharmed as the ceiling collapsed behind them. Children volunteered to crawl through the rubble to look for anyone who may have been trapped; no one was found. The Waller would not reopen.

1920–1967: Park Theatre

In her book *The Silver Screen*, Marjorie McNinch mentions the Park went through "sporadic film schedules" before closing in December after a screening of *Up the Down Staircase*.

FADE OUT

As society worked toward ensuring film lovers of all races had equal access to all theaters, it also continued working toward deeming the appropriateness of the content of the films played by those theaters. While the latter wasn't new, it certainly created a curious juxtaposition in the wake of the civil rights movement: all people should be allowed to go to the movies, but only those movies some people think all people should be allowed to see. But just as the late 1960s began the movement of films with greater sexual content, the same timeframe continued with increased conservative resistance to that content. Neither side would yield anytime soon.

LOST AND FOUND

Lost theater memories can be found around the state if you know where to look.

An original spool of Reese Theatre tickets, circa 1960. This is available to view at the Greater Harrington Historical Society. *Photo by Victoria Nazarewycz.*

TAKE 10
THE 1970s

Of Movies, Sex and the Multiplex

FADE IN

With a century in the books, the evolution of film exhibition in Delaware through the 1960s is most easily tracked in terms of technology, from magic lanterns to moving pictures, from silent movies to sound, from flickering black-and-white to vibrant color, from a single dimension to three and from finding a parking spot near the walk-in theater to parking your car in front of the screen at the drive-in. But over that century, every one of the approximately 122 theaters that showed movies in this state, regardless of time, town, technology or tenure, all had one thing in common: they showed their movies on a single screen. Not anymore. The birthrate of theaters may have been slowing, but the multiplication of screens was booming.

OPENING CREDITS

Concord Mall Cinema | 1970–1980
Concord Mall Twin | 1980–1989
AMC Concord Mall II/2 | 1989–1999
(Wilmington)

The 850-seat Concord Mall Cinema, located on Route 202 in the northern suburbs of Wilmington, opened not unlike the downtown movie houses of old, with live music, Kliegl lights and a personal appearance by the premiering film's producer/star. That talent was William Bryant, and his theater-opening film was *The Outdoorsman*, a nature documentary that drew blistering criticism from the *News Journal* for its glorified depiction of the hunting and killing of animals. The review went so far as to compare the documentary's violence to *Bonnie and Clyde*, *The Wild Bunch* and the Zapruder film. The theater opened as a single screen and would remain a single for the decade.

Sussex West Drive-In | 1970–1983
Super 13 Drive-In | 1983–circa 1986
(Laurel)

Without a theater since the Waller closed in 1967, the town of Laurel was treated to its own drive-in by Richard Derrickson. In August, the four-hundred-car open-air theater debuted with a Disney double feature of *The Boatniks* and *Blackbeard's Ghost*. The theater would also feature live rock shows in the decade.

Branmar Cinema | 1970–1980
AMC Branmar Twin/2 | 1980–circa 1991
(Wilmington)

Another strip mall theater opened in the northern suburbs of Wilmington in 1970: the Schwartz-owned Branmar Cinema, located in the Branmar Shopping Center at the corner of Marsh and Silverside Roads. The single-screen theater had a whirlwind first decade, invoking traits of many of its downtown predecessors. Its opening, while not as flashy as Concord Mall's, featured better fare (the star-studded thriller *Airport*) along with a chance to win two tickets to any "airport" in the United States. Throughout the decade it hosted benefits, screened the locally produced seven-minute short film *The Bold Poachers* (Arden Films), upped its gimmick game with screenings of *Earthquake* in Sensurround, treated customers to the classics and even dabbled in adult stuff with titles like *The Oral Generation*. But perhaps its best story (ever, really) was the time Hollywood royalty almost screened his own film there.

In 1977, Clint Eastwood directed and starred in the gritty crime thriller *The Gauntlet*. The film was slated to be released in December, but Eastwood wanted a test screening in October and wanted to sit in a theater unbeknownst to the audience, to get their honest reaction to it. The circumstances surrounding the selection of the Branmar are a little vague, but it was chosen at least in part because it was close to New York and Eastwood's Connecticut home, and the star wanted to avoid being recognized in a larger city.

The sneak preview was only advertised the day of the screening, as producers were looking to avoid too large a crowd that would (naturally) be interested in a sneak peek at the latest Eastwood flick. The plan yielded only a handful of people instead—so few, in fact, the disguised Eastwood left the theater before the film started. His costar, Sondra Locke, sat through the film unrecognized.

In 1979, the Schwartz family sold the Branmar to Budco, who had designs on twinning the theater.

Tri-State Mall Theater | 1970–1983
Eric Tri-State Mall | 1983–1994
Cinemagic 5 | 1994–1998
Tri-State Theaters | circa 1999
(Claymont)

And then the multiplex was born. The Tri-State Mall Theater was the first multiple-screen theater in the state, but being a twin wasn't in the original plan.

In 1968, Sameric Theaters announced it would open a single-screen 1,400-seat movie theater in Claymont's brand new Tri-State Mall by the end of the year, but the company changed direction, and some two years later, on November 11, 1970, the Eric I premiered, offering both thirty-five- and seventy-millimeter projection, a sixty-foot panoramic screen, high fidelity stereophonic sound and the latest in rocking seats, 1,200 in all. The opening film was *Lovers and Other Strangers*. Six weeks later, just in time for Christmas, its smaller twin, weighing in at 650 seats, the Eric II, opened with *Scrooge*, the holiday musical starring Albert Finney. The theater was just warming up (and I don't mean thanks to its screening of the X-rated *Last Tango in Paris* in 1973).

On May 25, 1977, two events occurred. The Tri-State Mall Theater opened the Eric III, and it became one of only forty-five theaters in the country, and the only theater in Delaware, to screen *Star Wars*. That latter distinction would last for more than a month.

Castle Mall King and Queen | 1971–1989
Loew's King and Queen | 1989–circa 1991
(Newark)

Another twin to appear in the state was a new build at the Castle Mall, located at the intersection of Chestnut Hill Road and South Chapel Street in Newark. Where the Tri-State Mall numbered its theaters to uniquely identify them, this new strip-mall denizen used names as the differentiator: one theater was the King, the other was the Queen. On that opening night in November, the Queen had two showings of *Kotch*. The King screened Oscar-winning Disney documentaries *The Living Desert* and *The Vanishing Prairie*.

The King and Queen, with only 325 seats per theater, was the first in a planned chain of thirty theaters of similar size and design by National Mini-Theaters. The strategy was to avoid the heavy up-front costs experienced by first-run cinemas by instead offering "quality second-run films, most of them general audience." (Its acquisition of the recently released *Kotch* for its open was last-minute good fortune.)

The King and Queen may have shown its share of adult films, but even as a second-run theater, it showed some winners. Such was the case in September 1972 when it screened *The Godfather*, which opened at first-run theaters in March of that year. *From the personal collection of JJ Garvine.*

But what set the theater apart from any other in the state was how each film was presented. Thanks to the Toshiba Photo Phone Company, the theater's film exhibition process was fully automated. Technicians from Japan oversaw the installation of the tape-run equipment that, once set, would drop the lighting and open the curtain before each film rolled, roll that film in the first projector, then switch to the second projector at the right time. The need for a pure projectionist was gone, as any trained employee could handle the rewinding of the film and/or trigger each day's start (at least in theory). In the event of technical difficulties, manual overrides were available and the equipment would shut down on its own if a film snapped. This kept staffing lean.

Of course, this marvel of technology was soon used to show pornography. Months after selling itself as the home of "quality second-run films, most of them general audience," the King and Queen took advantage of its dual-screen structure by frequently playing a mainstream picture on one screen and something X-rated on the other. The practice began in early 1972, but a striking example of how willing the theater was to run these screenings in parallel could be found in December 1974, when the Queen showed Disney's *Dumbo* and *Herbie Rides Again*, but the King screened *Bordello* and *Doctor, I'm Coming*. It is unconfirmed whether anyone was ever directed to the wrong room.

Towne Cinema | 1972–circa 1983
First State Theater/First State Art Cinema | circa 1984
(Dover)

Dover's next movie theater was a little place that opened with little fanfare. At three hundred seats, the Towne continued the trend of mini-theaters and was the first of that type in the state capital. Its opening picture was *The New Centurions*.

Triangle Mall Cinema | 1972–circa 1981
The Square | circa 1981–circa 1985
Music Makers Theatre | circa 1985–circa 1987
New Castle Square | circa 1987–circa 1988
New Castle Mall | circa 1988–circa 1989
Loew's New Castle Mall | circa 1989–circa 1991
Loew's New Castle Square | circa 1991–circa 1992
(New Castle)

For a theater that advertised under so many names in its relatively short lifespan, there is little to tell about it. Part of the National Mini-Theater chain (like the King and Queen), this strip mall twin featured 325 seats in each auditorium. It bowed in late December and offered *What's Up Doc?* and *Fiddler on the Roof* for its grand opening. But like its Newark sister, the Triangle quickly moved into adult screenings, including *It Happened in Hollywood* the year following its opening.

Twin Oaks Drive-In | 1973–1979
(Cheswold)

Just north of Dover, Richard Derrickson expanded with the Twin Oaks Drive-In, but the theater never really took off. Derrickson cited a combination of issues that sealed the theater's fate, including a lack of good product (Blaxploitation, martial arts and hard-R films were the norm), the location, the lack of an entrance from the main highway, the rise of unemployment driving down attendance and the fact that drive-ins were on the decline. The short-lived Twin Oaks was the last new drive-in to open in the state and lived for only six years.

Seaford Twin Cinema | 1973–1993
(Seaford)

In April 1973, with the single-screen Layton as the only theater in town, Seaford found itself part of the multiscreen craze with the Seaford Twin in the Ames Shopping Center, courtesy of Wilson Theaters. The five-hundred-seat theater opened with the musical *1776* and Disney's *Snowball Express*. It would soon delve into adult films, including *The Devil in Miss Jones* in January 1974.

Chestnut Hill 2 | 1973–circa 1988
AMC Chestnut Hill 2 | circa 1988–circa 1990
AMC Chestnut 2 | circa 1990–1993
Chestnut Hill Cinema Cafe | 1994–circa 1996
(Newark)

Next up for the sprawling suburb of Newark was the Chestnut Hill 2. The twins in the standalone building located in the Chestnut Hill Plaza were originally to have been named the Plaza I and II. Wilson Theaters, owner of the months-old Seaford Twin, was behind this theater as well. Live festivities were held before the opening screenings of *Battle for the Planet of the Apes* and *Man of La Mancha*, and in 1974, the theater participated in a French film festival. That said, hosting such highbrow fare didn't stop the theater from showing adult films like other twins before it, such as its 1976 screening of *Emmanuelle: The Joys of a Woman* (an X-rater at the time that has since been tamed to an NC-17).

Milford Plaza Cinema | 1973–circa 1983
(Milford)

Wilson Theaters scored the hat trick with its third 1973 theater, the Milford Plaza Cinema. Unlike its siblings, this theater was a 350-seat *single*, but following the path begun by the King and Queen, its projection system was fully automated. It opened in late September with *Paper Moon*, and in early October, it offered children's matinees, starting with the animated *Charlotte's Web*.

Cinema 273 | 1973–circa 1988
(Newark)

A month later, back in Newark, another strip-mall single opened. It would be the town's sixth open theater in total and its fourth new theater in five years. Cinema 273, located in University Plaza on Route 273, had its open delayed when a Long Island warehouse suffered a sprinkler malfunction, soaking all three hundred theater seats that were awaiting shipment. Instead of *Live and Let Die* on October 11, the theater opened with *Tom Sawyer* on October 25.

Within a year, due to lack of sales borne of an inability to book competitive films, its owners sold to Universal Theaters Inc., a company affiliated with seventeen adult theaters in Philadelphia. Not surprisingly, Cinema 273 changed programming to all-adult content, and that was met with success. At least for the next few years, the theater was, in the words of the *Morning News*, the "best-run and most successful X-rated theater in the state."

Still, there was a swell of moral resistance, and in 1978, a group called Stamp Out Smut picketed outside the shopping center with signs reading *X Movies Must Go* and *God Hates Porn*. They handed out pamphlets with scripture and misleading clichés about porn and porn viewers to drivers willing to slow down and engage them. Once again, a theater found itself at the center of a greater societal morality conflict.

Christiana Mall Cinema | 1979–2002
AMC Christiana Mall | 2002
(Newark)

The last theater to open in the state in the 1970s became Newark's fourth to open in the decade, its fifth to open over the previous ten years and its seventh open theater overall, and its attachment to a new shopping mall, as well as the fact it planned to open as a triple (the first in the state intended to begin as a three-screener), certainly helped the Christiana Mall Cinema's chances for success. But being part of a greater structure came with its own challenges.

The theater's construction was complete, but it would be four months before it finally opened because of an unexpected problem: noise level—not from its own theaters, but from the live music playing in the adjacent Duke's Pub. Theater owner General Cinemas decided to open two of the three screens at the mall while engineers worked to improve the soundproofing on the remainder of the completed construction. Their opening films were *Yanks* and *Just You and Me Kid*.

MOVING PICTURES

The stories of the decade can be divided into two groups: obscenities-related stories and everything else. I'll cover everything else first—it's actually quicker.

In 1971, the state saw its second twin. Mere months after the new Tri-State Mall twin opened at the north end of the state, the Midway Palace, at the southern end in Rehoboth, opened its second screening room in April. It wouldn't be that theater's last screen, nor would it be that company's last theater, as owner Richard Derrickson acquired the Layton Theatre in Seaford.

In 1973, the Grand and the Clayton celebrated reopenings (of sorts). The former was remodeled and reopened, kicking off its new season with the Cleveland Orchestra but soon after hosting a series of foreign films in partnership with the Delaware Art Museum. The latter, which had gone out of business in late 1972, was purchased and reopened around Christmas of '73. And it was sometime around then that the Smyrna Theatre closed for several years for reasons undetermined. At the midpoint of the decade, the Rehoboth Art League hosted a film festival at the Midway Palace, and Budco bought Cinemart (the second time in two years that theater changed hands).

Ah, 1977. Sure, Clint Eastwood almost saw a film at Branmar. Yes, twins were sprouting up around the state (while Tri-State birthed a triplet). Indeed, the Lewes Theater was sold and became the Lewes Cinema, abandoning

On the left of this 1971 photo is the Midway Palace, in the Midway shopping center, at the time merely a twin (it would someday become the fourteen-screen Movies at Midway). In the upper right-hand corner, behind the shopping center, is the Midway Drive-In. *Courtesy of the Derrickson family.*

X-rated content to embrace foreign and art house films. But really, *Star Wars* was the main thing of consequence during the year, and rightfully so. After Tri-State enjoyed more than a month of exclusivity screening the film (which would go on to play there for most of the rest of the year), the film phenom spread throughout the state.

In 1978, while Cinema 141 was joining the crowd and splitting into two theaters, the owner of the building in which the State Theatre resided refused to renew the lease, citing the leaseholder had been "unsatisfactory." The theater had struggled to compete with area chains to win the rights to screen new releases. With that, the State closed, but the building owner was willing to allow the theater to reopen under new management. It didn't take long for that new life to be found. Newark's oldest existing theater reopened in February 1979 and did so with the gusto only a thirty-one-hour movie marathon could supply. Working in concert with Philadelphia's TLA, the

State planned to fill a Delaware film void by becoming a repertory cinema, offering films found at no other theater around.

Also, in Smyrna, the years-dormant Smyrna Theatre reopened as a live venue, while in Dover, the Dover Cinema pulled a page from theaters' old playbooks and offered a Christmastime double feature for kids: *Run for Your Life Charlie Brown* and *Bad News Bears Go to Japan*. Just like the old days, a ticket cost one can of food for charity.

There is one final story from the Everything Else file. The Schwartz family got out of the movie theater business in 1979, selling nearly all its Delaware (and Maryland) theaters. The only two properties the Schwartz family retained were the Smyrna and Everett, neither of which they had designs on making/keeping as movie theaters and the latter of which closed in 1979. The Everett, having burned down twice and having gone out of business once already, had again come to an end. But just as the theater was no stranger to struggle, it was no stranger to survival either. Its comeback was on the horizon.

As for obscenities and the 1970s, the battle of high morals versus free speech wasted no time getting underway in the decade. The opening shot rang out in Wilmington in January 1970 when Mayor Harry Haskell signed an anti-obscenity ordinance into law. In short, anyone could file an obscenities complaint, and if probable cause was shown, a warrant would be served and the City Solicitor's Office would supply "expert testimony on whether or not [what was reported] is obscene." The final decision would then be left to the courts. The owner of Wilmington's Rialto, Richard Lewis, was eventually charged with violating the ordinance. Police raided his theater and confiscated a reel of film containing coming attractions for four films: *Love Now, Pay Later*; *Spiked Heels and Black Nylons*; *Ride, Mister?*; and *Potpourri*. Only the latter two would be named as offenders. Lawsuits and counter-lawsuits were filed into 1971 and the case almost made it to the U.S. Supreme Court, but that judicial body declined to hear it. In the end, a lower court ordered that the trailers confiscated by the city could be retained by the city.

As this was going on, Wilmington faced a curious test of its law in March 1970 when Allen Funt (of TV's *Candid Camera*) released the film *What Do You Say to a Naked Lady?*, an X-rated hidden camera film that puts everyday clothed people in awkward and unexpected social situations with naked people. When it was released in Delaware, all eyes were on Wilmington not only because of its new law but also because the film was released by a major distributor (United Artists) and was screening at a major theater

(Loew's Aldine), so there was curiosity about how the city would handle an opponent with a little more heft than the Rialto. After no arrests or closures had occurred at the Loew's Aldine, the city solicitor claimed he had received no *citizen* complaints about the film so he took no action (even though reports claimed he had vice cops routinely looking for infractions at the Rialto).

New Castle County wasn't alone in wrestling with these dilemmas. In February 1970, Lewes Theater manager Wilson Cullum was arrested for showing *Love Me...Please!*, a film deemed obscene and thus confiscated. Later in the year, the charges were dropped for the same reason the charges against the manager of the now-closed Milton Theatre (who screened *Motel Confidential* in the late 1960s) had been dropped: a judge cited federal precedent that prohibited the submission of evidence deemed as obscene solely based on the opinion of a police officer.

But for all the drama that had happened in 1970 and 1971, including refunds offered by the Cinema Center for people who were offended by *A Clockwork Orange* (X-rated on its original release), only two words mattered in Delaware film exhibition and theatergoing in 1972: *Deep Throat*.

The infamous adult film found its summertime way to the First State, and its first theater (at least in New Castle County) was Cinema 141, followed by the Edge Moor (which had drifted away from its higher-regarded foreign fare). The film was a massive success, the benefactor of burning curiosity across all demographics, general increased interest in adult entertainment, a high-quality product (comparatively) and a dearth of quality moneymaking mainstream films around the state—and around the state is where *Deep Throat* made its way.

One stop was in Newark at the State Theatre, much to the dismay of town councilmen, who requested the theater never show any X-rated films again; the theater declined that request. (Oddly, the State had shown adult films before with no interference. It was the combination of sex and popularity that seemed to drive the townsmen to approach the theater.)

Days later, at the Delmar Drive-In (2), Muriel Schwartz was ordered by the Delaware Attorney General's Office to not show the film. She complied on opening night, then defied the night after that. The attorney general was concerned that minors not admitted to the theater would still be able to see the action on the screen from outside the theater's perimeter, now a violation of state law (an issue the Newark Drive-In had contended with in 1970 with the Funt film). Schwartz acquiesced so as to avoid having employees arrested, but she was in consult with her attorneys. The film was also playing at her Capitol Theatre in Dover, as well as at the Lewes Theater.

In Newark, things were heating up as the Pike Creek Christian Coalition, a consortium of five churches, backed Newark's councilmen in their position of wanting to ban the exhibition of X-rated films. Town council considered passing a law, but members were concerned it wouldn't stick. Things were also getting hot in Dover. The city had passed its own obscenity ordinance (albeit one it couldn't really enforce, since similar laws were tied up in courts), while at the state level, the idea of a censorship board was proposed in lieu of more legislation.

The next few years saw even more action and reaction. The Capitol played a film called *Teenage Fantasies*, but Dover lawmakers weren't having it. With a new obscenities ordinance in place, four warrants were issued for the arrest of Muriel Schwartz, one for each time the theater played the latest X-rater. City officials also threatened one new warrant for every time the film was subsequently shown, and they sought to ban the theater from playing the film at all. Schwartz refused to stop screening the film, and by the time the case made it to court, the film had already left the theater as part of the natural turnover of film exhibition. After more legal wrangling, Schwartz was fined and intended to appeal.

Her position had always been one of a shrewd businesswoman. Her theaters weren't in the X-rated game the way places like the Rialto were; her philosophy was truly about supply and demand. During her case, she cited attendance figures (numbers she was known to keep guarded) to prove her point. She showed the court that in the first two days she screened Disney's *Run, Cougar, Run* and *The Misadventures of Merlin Jones*, she sold 24 tickets. For her first two days of *Teenage Fantasies*, she sold 1,011. While results may have been different at other theaters around the state, Schwartz's numbers represented the kind of pull X-rated movies had in the early '70s, and her stance not only as a businesswoman but also as a champion for freedom of speech made her the face of the cause.

Countering the trend, the Diamond State Drive-In shifted its programming *away* from adult fare and back toward mainstream movies, shortly before it was set to host what was thought to be a first in the state: a five-film dusk-to-dawn marathon of X-raters. The theater also changed its name to the Hiway 13 Drive-In. While all of this was going on, the U.S. Supreme Court decided, in a 5–4 ruling, it was up to the states to define what was obscene.

With that 1973 decision by the U.S. Supreme Court, Delaware wasted no time penning its own obscenities law, and within a week, that law was challenged by Budco Quality Theaters, owners of Cinema 141, the Concord Mall Cinema, the Edge Moor and the drive-ins at Naamans Road, Prices

The Smyrna Theatre briefly reopened around 1979. When it did, the Hunt Room that was once available for screenings of a more private nature was still there. Painted Stave Distillery, current resident of the building that once housed the theater, has left that room mostly untouched. Even the wallpaper remains, so the memories of Dickie and Cathy and David and Bonnie (*inset*) live on. *Photo by Victoria Nazarewycz.*

Corner and Pleasant Hill. They would also go on to fight the law prohibiting the exhibition of R- and X-rated movies by drive-ins where screens could be seen from the road. That law remained in limbo for years, and Budco almost tested its limits at Naamans. It had advertised it would screen the X-rated *The Story of Joanna* (as part of a double feature with the R-rated *Teenage Intimacies*), and when state prosecutor Charles Oberly caught wind, he reached out to Budco. Since the law was poorly written, Oberly had a handshake deal with drive-ins like Naamans, agreeing to not halt screenings of R-rated films in exchange for theaters voluntarily refraining from screening X-raters. Budco contended *Joanna* had been edited down to an R (despite advertising it as an X) but upon further consideration pulled the double feature entirely and instead played *Jaws* and *The Longest Yard*.

The Rialto, the X-rated movie house that became the poster child for the city's crusade against pornography, closed out the decade in ironic fashion. Manager Richard Lewis found Jesus and converted the theater to what he called the Mission Temple. Religious services were held there, and at least one faith-themed film, *Born Again*, was screened. The idea didn't take, and Lewis closed his place in June 1979.

CLOSING CREDITS

1915–1970: The Polonia | Avenue Theatre | Ace Theatre | Capri Art Theater

The Capri Art Theater, after seven years of screening adult fare and surviving pickets organized by the local parish, finally closed its doors in February 1970, accused of violating the city's newly minted obscenities law. The final screenings there were *Papagallo*, a film distributed by a San Francisco company specializing in adult films, and *99 Women*, a women-in-prison film. The owner closed rather than fight, as he felt he was deemed guilty until proven innocent and could not afford to defend every potential accusation leveled against him.

1921–1970: The Aldine | Loew's Aldine

Falling just short of fifty years in business, Loew's Aldine closed, citing poor attendance and the looming expense of a new air-conditioning unit needed to stay open in the summer months. Once closed, only the Grand, the Rialto and the Warner remained open downtown (as of 1970).

1922–1972: Plaza Theatre | New Plaza Theatre | Schine's New Plaza Theatre | Community Plaza Theatre | Milford Theatre/Schine's New Milford Theatre

After being sold in the late 1960s, the Milford Theatre closed sometime in 1972 following a screening of *Straw Dogs*. It would reopen later in the decade for live shows only, and in 1980, it became the Jesus Love Temple.

1938–circa 1974: Ball Theatre

Huck Betts, who retired from Major League Baseball to become a theater owner, retired from theater ownership in 1973 and sold the Ball Theatre to Coastal Cinema Corporation, which leased the building for a year. The last film listing I found was *Foxy Brown* in September 1974, a point in time that aligns with a one-year lease.

1906–1975: Moving Picture Place | Melodium | Nickelodeon | Savoy | Towne Theatre

After closing in 1967, Wilmington's Towne Theatre reopened in 1973 when its lease was assumed from RKO-Stanley Warner and it passed all necessary inspections. It was cited there was a demand for a downtown theater where people could take their children. However, martial arts and Blaxploitation movies, as well as pornography, eventually became the norm. The theater closed for good in 1975.

1919–1977: Royal Theatre | Elaine Theatre | Colonial Theatre | Earle Theatre

As the decade progressed, a combination of factors forced John and Grace Kozak to consider selling New Castle's Earle Theatre, the place they bought in 1941. Television was one factor, but so too were things like the inability to outbid chain theaters for new movies, an uptick in utility rates and even increased newspaper ad rates. Plus, the Kozaks were insistent on avoiding R- and X-rated films. When times got harder, they ran the theater on their own, with Grace selling tickets and popcorn and John running the projectors. They even lived in an apartment above the theater. It wasn't enough, and they put the place up for sale. Grace passed away in 1978, John in 1985.

1949–circa 1977: Brandywine Drive-In | Ellis Drive-In

Another decade, another theater and another arrest, although this one had nothing to do with obscenities. In 1972, the manager of the Ellis was arrested for running a major fencing operation from the theater, which appears to have closed about five years later. The last listing, in November 1977, was a double feature of *Orca* and *King Kong*.

1939–1977: Warner Theatre

The year 1970 brought one of the last truly unique events to the Warner: a simulated fight between Rocky Marciano and Muhammad Ali. A very smart sports enthusiast by the name of Murry Woroner had entered thousands of facts about various fighters into a computer, and he staged simulated fights among them until only one remained standing: Marciano. The problem? Woroner didn't include Ali in those simulations. One thing led to another, and Marciano and Ali—the former having retired due to age and the latter having retired due to issues with the government—got back in shape and "acted" the fight the computer scripted for them, all for film cameras. Five different endings were filmed, and only Woroner knew the outcome. That film—*The Super Fight*—was screened at about five hundred theaters in North America, including the Warner. (Marciano won.)

But there wasn't enough magic left in the theater to keep it running much longer. Like so many other fading movie houses, the Warner's cinematic offerings had been reduced to exploitation films and porn. In 1973, RKO-Stanley Warner sold the theater. The only manager the theater ever knew, Lewis Black, who opened the place in 1939, retired with the sale. The theater would remain open for a few more years, offering some films and live shows, but it was a shell of the once glorious movie house it used to be.

1946–1978: Center Theatre

The Center Theatre, having served the community and tourists of Rehoboth for more than thirty years, closed after Labor Day weekend 1978. This left Rehoboth Avenue with only one theater, the Beachwood.

1962–1979: Prices Corner Drive-In

The shelf life of drive-ins was starting to expire by the late 1970s. Of the state's original fifteen, only ten remained at the start of 1979. By year's end, that number dropped to nine with the closure of the Price's Corner Drive-In. Even after allowing its lot to be used for car sales in the off-season, the theater rolled its last double feature in September: *Star Wars* and *Battlestar Galactica*. The owner, Budco, made the conscious decision not to renew the lease.

FADE OUT

The 1970s were a decade of growth and growing pains.

Growth came in two forms: theaters and screens. A net increase of three theaters were in place at the end of 1979 when compared to the same time in 1969—up from thirty-six to thirty-nine. But the growth of screens experienced a much larger boost, with new builds being mostly twins, with existing singles expanding to pairs and with the birth of two triplets. The price paid, however, was an increasing number of smaller rooms.

As for growing pains, the limits of art, the limits of tolerance and the limits of the law were tested and retested, echoing sentiments of decades past, but dealing with films that were more advanced than ever before. The conclusion of that battle was looming.

HISTORIC MOVIE THEATERS OF DELAWARE

LOST AND FOUND

Lost theater memories can be found around the state if you know where to look.

The seats in the left photo were once a part of the Clayton Theatre. They can still be found there, but for display purposes only. *Photo by Victoria Nazarewycz.*

This projector is on display at the Clayton Theatre and can be seen, along with other memorabilia, as you make your way to the theater's balcony. Another projector just like it is in the projection booth. Most film screenings are now digital, but thirty-five-millimeter is a viable option there. *Photo by Victoria Nazarewycz.*

TAKE 11
THE 1980s

The Decade of Downsizing

FADE IN

Even when theaters worked closely together for a specific cause (e.g., during the 1940s to aid the war effort), they were still in direct competition with one another and using whatever they could to get an advantage over the other guy: title selection, technological advances, contests and more. Even the very construct of the drive-in theater was a gimmick by way of exhibition, enticing people to the movies without them having to leave their cars, get babysitters, primp and so on. Twins and triples were a similar gimmick, albeit by way of variety; if a customer didn't like what was in Theater A, there were other options in Theaters B and C. The field of play wasn't always level (chains stood a better chance of scoring better films), but each exhibitor did what it could to do better than the other exhibitors.

That was through the 1970s. The 1980s brought a new kind of competition to theaters: the home. TV had mostly been an alternative to moviegoing, but in the '80s, the boom of premium cable and the VCR turned the small screen into a personal exhibitor, bringing full-length feature films directly to the home, without commercials, and while not "on demand" as we know it today, certainly more so than waiting for a favorite new release to show up on a major network once a year. Home viewing would never truly mimic the in-theater experience, but it offered an economy and convenience that theater exhibition could not compete with.

This, combined with the other usual factors (poor management, rising costs, bad luck and so forth), decimated the theatrical landscape in 1980s Delaware. The decade began with thirty-nine theaters. It would lose nearly half those by the end of 1989, at an average rate of almost two per year.

OPENING CREDITS

Movies 6 | 1981–1990
Fox Movies 6 | 1990–1996
Carmike Movies 6 | 1996-circa 2000
(Dover)

Movies 6, in Dover's Rodney Village Shopping Center, wasted no time raising the multi-screen stakes when it became the first new build to start with six screens. It opened the first four on July 17, offering a nice variety: the latest James Bond flick, *For Your Eyes Only*; *The Great Muppet Caper* for the kids; *Clash of the Titans* for the sword-and-sandals set; and the great comedy *Arthur*. It opened the other two screens on July 24 with R-raters *Wolfen* and the Bo Derek vehicle *Tarzan, the Ape Man*. Flexing its tech, all six projectors were fully automated.

Rehoboth Twin Cinema | 1983–1988
(Rehoboth Beach)

The Rehoboth Twin Cinema brought movies back to Rehoboth Avenue for the first time in three years (the Beachwood closed in 1980; see Closing Credits), but the venture only lasted until 1988. It was the shortest tenure for a new theater in forty years. It was also the first multiplex to close.

Fox Cinema/The Fox | 1983–1996
Carmike Dover | 1996–1999
Carmike 14 | 1999–2017
AMC CLASSIC Dover 14 | 2017–present
(Dover)

Reading, Pennsylvania–based Fox Theaters owned every public movie theater in the state capital: aging single-screeners Towne Cinema, Blue Hen Mall Theater, Capitol Theatre and Kent Drive-In (all of which it acquired from the Schwartz family). Fox had also recently opened the city's first multiplex with Movies 6 in Rodney Village. In December 1983, it added another six screens to its tally when it opened the Fox Cinema inside Dover Mall.

Baymart Cinema | 1988–1993
(Rehoboth Beach)

Richard Derrickson had designs on opening another Rehoboth theater. Off-street parking was a hot topic for merchants along Rehoboth Avenue, so he instead converted an old National 5&10 Cent Store in the Bay Mart Shopping Center into a four-screener. It was a seasonal theater that struggled as merchants left the shopping center due to dwindling business lost to newer, year-round shopping centers just north of downtown Rehoboth.

Riverfront Theater | 1989–present
(Milford)

Originally opened as a venue for live performances, the Riverfront Theater in Milford is home to the Second Street Players. Prior to the open of the theater, the troupe, which dates to 1980, performed at places like Milford Middle School, Milford High and the J.C. Penney Building.

MOVING PICTURES

Although there was no new build in 1980, theaters continued to expand by way of increased screen count. The Christiana Mall Cinema finally opened that third screen, the split at Branmar also happened (as did the theater's rename to the AMC Branmar Twin) and the Concord Mall Cinema briefly closed so it could be split as well.

More changes in the landscape came in 1981. Before Movies 6 opened its half-dozen screens, the Midway Palace was the state leader in number of screens when its triple blossomed to a quintet in May. Back north, Delaware's first original multiplex at the Tri-State Mall Theater moved from three screens to four. The once-closed Rialto, which had ended its run in 1979 as the Mission Temple, was born again, with the intent to show foreign and art house films.

Finding its way back to the hard stuff, the Hiway 13 Drive-In did what it had intended to do when it was called the Diamond State but didn't get the chance before the name and content changes: the theater held a dusk-to-dawn porn marathon, screening six titles across the night: *Good Girls of Godiva High*; *Pastries*; *Easy*; *For Richer, For Poorer*; *How Sweet It Is*; and *Prisoner of Love*.

It was quite a range of events for a trio of legacy theaters in 1982. Like a good sequel, the Everett returned, this time purchased from the Schwartz family by the community organization ACT (Association of Community Talent), led by Ellen Combs Davis, a longtime theater patron. Live music, plays and eventually movies would resume. The Grand held a nine-film Summer Film Festival, playing mostly classics (including *The Sound of Music*, *The Day the Earth Stood Still* and *Young Frankenstein*). But the Capitol, formerly the Dover Opera House, had fallen into disrepair and closed.

There also was a lot of movement elsewhere in the first half of the decade. The Christiana Mall expanded from three to five screens (ironically, those two new screens occupied the space that once housed Duke's Pub, the source of the theater's previous sound woes). The Seaford Twin, Milford Plaza, Layton, Sussex West and Chestnut Hill Twin were all sold to various buyers. The Tri-State Mall Theater became the Eric Tri-State Mall and opened its fifth screen, and the Midway Palace expanded to six screens from five, then expanded again and quietly became the state's largest multiplex with seven screens. It's a title the theater would hold for the rest of the decade.

If you can't beat 'em, join 'em, so the saying goes, and that's pretty much what the Clayton Theatre did in 1985 when it opened Silver Screen Video next door. The video rental store, riding the wave of home video popularity, offered new releases and hard-to-find classics, as well as VCR rentals. To the best of my knowledge, this is the only case of a theater/video store combo in the state's history. It also appears that the Dover Cinema closed around this time, or at least films stopped showing there.

A pair of drive-ins in the state had different types of near-miss closures in 1986. The Hiway 13 Drive-In returned to its original name (Diamond State) but to none of its original glory and folded. The Naamans Drive-In also thought it closed that year—what it didn't know is that it had one good year left in it. In 1987, AMC purchased Budco, which in Delaware included the acquisition of the Concord Mall Twin, the Cinema Center and the Chestnut Hill Cinema. In Kent County, the Dover Cinema reopened as the Blue Hen Mall Theater, specializing in live music (and possibly films). In 1988, Cinema 141 became the AMC Cinema 141.

In Newark in 1989, the Castle Mall King and Queen became the Loews King and Queen, and in Kent County, the Dover Cinema's tenure as the Blue Hen Mall Theater was short-lived. It changed names again to the Blue Hen Mall Concert Hall. Across the decade, the Triangle Mall Cinema went through its long series of name changes.

No decade would be complete without a major story; the 1980s offered two.

The first had a familiar beat: morality. Back in 1977, a law had been passed intended to regulate and issue licenses to certain adult establishments. With that law came the formation of the Delaware Commission on Massage Establishments and Adult Bookstores. The poorly written law had less than its intended effect, so new legislation was passed in 1980, and the committee was renamed the Commission of Adult Entertainment Establishments. The new law still included massage parlors and bookstores in its scope, but the list was expanded to include peep shows, topless bars and movie theaters. Its initial focus was not on movie theaters.

That changed in 1982. In November, the manager of the Delmar Drive-In (2) appears to have been the first theater-related person arrested for violating the law when he screened a pornographic film without a license. This was the first shot fired. The next shot was aimed at the State Theatre in Newark.

On December 2, the State received a warning that employees might be arrested if the adult double bill of *Debbie Does Dallas* and *Insatiable* was presented without the theater being licensed. Rather than face the potential for a $500 fine or six months in jail (or both), State owner Barry Solan agreed to close for the night, although he was quick to accuse authorities of selectively targeting him, citing they would have to drive past the X-rated movies at the Cinema Center to get to his theater. Solan, whose application had been filed but not yet processed, had a greater argument against needing a license, calling out the fact that his was not an adult entertainment establishment, but a movie theater playing films from a wide variety of genres and that the adult films he played represented less than 10 percent of his total screenings.

The ripple effect was swift. The Cinema Center and the Tri-State Mall, both of which were set to show adult films, pulled those titles for fear of legal ramifications and replaced them with R-rated movies instead. (These theaters were showing adult films as "filler"—something to fill the screening schedule while waiting for better mainstream films closer to Christmas.)

The situation at Cinema 273 was a little different. Since porn was its sole product, it had a license, but it had expired. Rather than tempt fate, the theater replaced *Seven Seductions* with *Rocky III*.

Solan recognized a flaw in the licensing law, at least as it applied to movie theaters. The law stated that once an adult entertainment license was issued to an establishment, no one under eighteen could ever enter that establishment. This wasn't an issue for places like adult bookstores and massage parlors, where kids wouldn't go anyway, but it played havoc with movie theaters that offered adult films as part of a broader program. Solan thought the law was unconstitutional, and he planned to test it, and test the committee, by screening a PG-rated movie and allowing teens to enter the theater to see it—but only *after* his license was approved. His publicly vocalized sentiment drew the ire of the committee, which delayed his application while it looked into whether it could deny the license based on having advance knowledge that the applicant was going to willfully break the law once licensed.

Not only was it ruled the license had to be granted (because the application was properly completed and the fee was paid), but the committee also indicated it would not arrest Solan if he allowed minors to view PG-rated films (at least not immediately). Before dispatching police, the committee wanted to ensure it was on firm constitutional grounds.

In 1983, the State Theatre prevailed. The portion of the law that stated children were prohibited from viewing suitable films simply because the same theater sometimes showed X-rated films was deemed unconstitutional (by violating each child's rights). Confusion about other portions of the law remained. Some theater owners (the out-of-town corporations) were unaware of the law, and local law enforcement was unsure exactly how to interpret it. For example, part of the law stated a theater needed a license if it showed a film with "less than completely opaquely covered" buttocks or female breasts. That description applies to many PG-rated films, let alone R- and X-raters. Lawmakers admitted when they crafted the law, their thinking was geared toward businesses that specialized in hardcore material. They had not considered mainstream films would also fit their definition or that mainstream theaters would show both types of films.

The back end of the decade brought a much more lighthearted story.

Over the course of Delaware's history, Hollywood came here for many reasons: movie premieres, contests, bond drives and more. But Hollywood never came to Delaware the way it came to Delaware in late 1988. That's when director Peter Weir and star Robin Williams descended on the First

The State Theatre used to mail to its customers a seasonal eight-page flyer spotlighting its upcoming program. This is one page from the winter of 1985. *From the author's personal collection.*

State to film *Dead Poets Society*, the first feature-length film to shoot entirely in the state. Set at an all-boys prep school in Vermont, the film tells the story of John Keating (Williams), an English teacher who inspires his students to approach poetry in refreshing and unorthodox ways; this upsets the older, stodgier faculty at the school.

The ten-week shoot, which used locals as extras (from around town and the region, many in high school and on Christmas break), spent the bulk of its time at St. Andrew's School in Middletown, as well as in Old New Castle. But a pivotal scene in the film, where Mr. Perry (Kurtwood Smith) goes to see his son, Neil (Robert Sean Leonard), perform in Shakespeare's *A Midsummer Night's Dream*, was filmed at the Everett Theatre, which was refurbished for the shoot. Other stars filming at the theater included Norman Lloyd, Ethan Hawke and Lara Flynn Boyle. It seems poetic that the town with the first theater to go on to screen films be a central point in a film.

However, if Middletown and the Everett Theatre were drunk from their brush with Hollywood in 1988, they felt the hangover in 1989. In something of a disappointing postscript, the Everett could not get its

On the set of Peter Weir's *Dead Poets Society* (1989), on Main Street in Middletown. The Everett Theatre was used for both interior and exterior scenes. *Courtesy of the Everett Theatre.*

Behind the scenes of Peter Weir's *Dead Poets Society* (1989), on Main Street in Middletown. *Courtesy of the Everett Theatre.*

Of all the seats in the Everett Theatre, only one is cushioned in black. That seat is where Robin Williams sat for his theater scene in *Dead Poets Society*. The seat was changed from red to black after Williams's passing in 2014. It can be used by anyone in attendance at any show. *Photo by Victoria Nazarewycz.*

own screening of the film. It premiered in New York City, played at the Christiana Mall Cinema as a sneak preview the next day and, when the film began its regular run the following weekend, played at Branmar in north Wilmington and the Fox in Dover. Even pricey benefit screenings were held elsewhere: a $50 benefit happened at Friends School and a $125–$250 benefit took place at the Museum of Natural History, both a week later. The greatest challenge the Everett faced was having nowhere to host a reception before and/or after the film—plus its projection and sound equipment needed upgrades (something the museum was willing to do to score its screening). Still, the filming was all quite the ride and something that is remembered and celebrated to this day.

CLOSING CREDITS

1908–1980: Lewes Auditorium | Lewes Theater | Lewes Cinema

In the summer of 1980, the Lewes Cinema, still referred to in some news items as the Lewes Theater, was yet another Delaware theater to see its run end by fire. In what is surely the greatest twist of irony in the state's theater history, the Lewes Cinema had been screening *Up in Smoke*.

1968–1980: Cinemart

Suffering five-figure losses per year since buying the theater, Budco closed the Cinemart in September 1980. A previous effort to split the theater into a twin was unsuccessful, and employees were notified of the closure just hours before it happened. The theater's final screening was *The Exterminator*.

1941–1980: Edge Moor Theatre

Three weeks after closing the Cinemart and following a screening of the horror film *Mother's Day*, Budco closed the Edge Moor, also for financial reasons.

Circa 1909–1980: Casino Moving Picture Theatre | Blue Hen Theatre | Beachwood Theatre

For the first time since the beginning of the century, downtown Rehoboth was without a movie theater. Richard Derrickson, who was expanding the number of screens at the Midway Palace outside of town, closed the Beachwood to make way for retail stores.

Circa 1921–circa 1981: Palace Theatre | Strand Theatre | Smyrna Theatre

After about sixty years in total, the Smyrna Theatre finally closed. Today, in its place stands the Painted Stave, a distillery that has honored the history of the theater by retaining original parts of it, including the neon sign outside, sconces (some that still hang) where the seating area was and that old Hunt Room.

Historic Movie Theaters of Delaware

1908–1982: Lyric Theatre | New Lyric | Lyric | Rialto Theatre

It was a noble effort, but in its first renewed year, the Rialto was a money-loser. By February 1982, new owner Barry Solan (of the State) knew it was clear the city had no appetite for his product. Sixty days later, Delaware's oldest continuous movie house, as well as the last remaining movie theater within city limits, was closed forever.

1953–circa 1982: Midway Drive-In

With little attention in the news, the Midway Drive-In closed around 1982. The last film listing from October 7 was a triple feature of *Beastmaster*, *Forced Vengeance* and *Penitentiary Part II*.

1973–circa 1983: Milford Plaza Cinema

About a year after its sale in 1982, the Milford Plaza Cinema closed. The last film listing in the newspaper was the teen T&A comedy *Getting It On*.

1950–circa 1984: Pleasant Hill Drive-In

After a final listing in the papers of a *Staying Alive/Flashdance/Classroom Teasers* triple feature on New Year's Day 1984, the Pleasant Hill Drive-In appeared in the papers no more. The screen was torn down in 1988.

1969–circa 1984: Newark Drive-In

Nine months after the disappearance of Pleasant Hill in papers, the Newark Drive-In stopped appearing as well. Its last advertised offering, on September 6, was the triple feature of *Flashpoint*, *Red Dawn* and *Brainstorm*.

1950–circa 1985: Delmar Drive-In (2)

No other theater in the state's history found itself in the crosshairs of controversy from its opening to its close quite the way Delmar Drive-In (2) did, from 1950s blue laws to 1980s adult entertainment establishment licensing. At the end, it appeared in film listings on September 8 and not again. That presumed last show was, of course, an adult double feature of *A Little Bit of Hanky Panky* and *Panty Raid*.

Historic Movie Theaters of Delaware

1972–circa 1984: Towne Cinema | First State Theater/First State Art Cinema

Part of the Fox theaters, the Towne went through changes in 1984 that couldn't save it. This included a name change around June to the First State Theater, then another name change in August to the First State Art Cinema with a change in programming akin to what the State was offering. It wouldn't see the end of the year.

1941–1984: Layton Theatre | Layton Cinema

After its sale in 1982, the Layton Theatre became the Layton Cinema but only lasted two more years. The last screening listed (oddly, again as the Layton Theatre) was a December showing of *A Christmas Story*.

1970–circa 1986: Sussex West Drive-In | Super 13 Drive-In

In 1983, the Sussex West Drive-In changed its name to the Super 13 Drive-In. Three years later, its final listing appeared in the papers: a comedy double feature of *Wise Guys* and *Running Scared*.

1953–circa 1986: Kent Drive-In

Like so many other theaters before it, particularly drive-ins, the Kent Drive-In ended its run quietly. Its last listed screening from September 1 was the horror double feature *Texas Chainsaw Massacre Part II* and *Gates of Hell*.

1929–1987: State Theatre

Just because the State Theatre won the fight against adult licensing didn't mean it was indestructible. Its reputation and regard as the only rep house in Delaware was greater than the actual audience that came to be a part of it, and the theater was losing money. Compounding that was a settlement owed to Walt Disney Productions for publicly screening some Disney films meant for private showings. With all of that, plus back rent, back taxes and other past due expenses, the State closed in July 1986.

Not long after, former projectionist and theater manager Bob Weir took over the place, but his task was daunting. The last audience at the last show (theater staple *The Rocky Horror Picture Show*) trashed the place from screen to concession stand. Weir had enough funding to reopen, and if he could get the place repaired, he had plans of keeping the same programming, plus adding live concerts, meeting space for civic groups and even a small art gallery for local talent. On Friday, August 8, the State came alive again with a screening of *Turtle Diary*, plus weekend midnight shows of the *Rocky Horror* sequel *Shock Treatment*.

In October, the theater hosted "State Aid," an all-day concert event to raise money for itself, featuring local musical acts. It wasn't enough, and Weir was forced to fold in November. In March 1987, the building's owner held a concert, under the State Theatre shingle, featuring Tommy Conwell and the Young Rumblers. It was the first of what was to be four concerts in 1987, but building inspectors required more safety renovations than the venue was worth. That concert was the last event at the State. Gone forever was Newark's oldest operating theater.

1968–1987: Naamans Drive-In

A funny thing happened to the Naamans Drive-In in 1986. It closed—except it didn't. After its final triple feature (and a great one) of *The Fly*, *Aliens* and *Big Trouble in Little China*, the theater was supposed to have closed for good to be converted into an industrial park. But due to delays in zoning and other approvals, the property owner knew it wouldn't be ready before September 1987. Rather than let the land sit dormant for a year, he leased it to AMC (growing in Delaware at the time) for one last season. On Sunday, September 27, after a (not quite as great) double feature of *Hellraiser* and *House II: The Second Story*, the Naamans Drive-In closed for good, not only bringing an end to its own run but also an end to the drive-in era in the state.

1973–circa 1988: Cinema 273

Just as the closing of the Naamans Drive-In brought an end to Delaware's drive-in era, the closure of Cinema 273 brought an end to Delaware's pornography era. When the theater closed, the state's last X-rated movie house closed, yet it did so with none of the fanfare it had received when it was picketed. Its last advertised screening in July was the double feature *Pleasure Maze* and *Burning Snow*.

FADE OUT

The 1980s was the roughest decade on Delaware's theatrical landscape. It was the first decade when no new theater was opened with an address in any part of Wilmington or any part of New Castle County. The year 1988 was the first since 1949 that a drive-in theater didn't exist in the state. While total screens hovered around fifty, the total of only twenty-three theaters at the end of the decade (including the Playhouse, the Candlelight and the Riverfront, which didn't screen films, and the Dover Air Force Base and the Shalimar, which didn't screen films for the general public) was the lowest in the state's history at the close of a given era since the end of 1899. And its net loss of sixteen theaters was the biggest single-decade drop by a wide margin; the next closest was the net loss of eight theaters in the 1960s.

The 1990s couldn't do worse, but they couldn't necessarily do better, either.

LOST AND FOUND

Lost theater memories can be found around the state if you know where to look.

These seats, which don't look remotely comfortable, were once the standard in the Palace Theatre in Smyrna. They are on display at the Smyrna Museum. *Photo by Victoria Nazarewycz.*

TAKE 12

THE 1990s

The Meh Decade

FADE IN

The fewest number of theaters to permanently close in a decade during the twentieth century was five, between 1940 and 1949, followed by six, between 1900 and 1909. The 1990s represented the third fewest closings at ten. That's the good news. The bad news? The 1990s also tied for fewest new openings with five (along with the 1930s and the 1980s). This, coupled with the absence of a major theme in the decade, made the '90s very quiet.

Who doesn't love popcorn at the movies? Well, not some folks circa 1990, when local AMC theaters were giving away this bumper sticker. Aversion to canola oil was their reason to shun cinema's favorite snack. *From the personal collection of JJ Garvine.*

OPENING CREDITS

Cinemark Movies 10 | 1991–present
(Wilmington)

The Midway Palace in Rehoboth surrendered its title as the state's largest multiplex when Cinemark arrived in October 1991 with Movies 10 in the First State Plaza. After twenty years, it was the first new theater with a Wilmington address (albeit in the suburbs), and it came with a lot of uncommon things (for the time), including computerized ticket stations (in addition to its outdoor box office), a game room, heart-healthy popcorn and THX sound. The theater opened with a slate of eleven films; two shared one auditorium.

Regal Peoples Plaza (Stadium 17) | 1992–present
(Newark)

Giving Movies 10 competition in the multiplex game was Regal Peoples Plaza, a ten-screen theater in Newark, just off Route 40. Like Movies 10, the theater offered arcade games, and like Movies 10, it offered eleven films in its ten-screen theater. Setting the Regal apart from the Cinemark competition, however, was its grand opening pricing: for its first week, Regal Peoples Plaza offered ninety-nine-cent tickets for every showing of every film. As the decade progressed, the theater expanded its screen count, first to thirteen by 1993, then to seventeen by the end of the decade, the highest count in the state.

Rehoboth Mall Cinema | 1993–2008
(Rehoboth Beach)

Richard Derrickson expanded his theatrical footprint with something that was common up north but had not been done at the beach: a multiplex inside a shopping mall. The six-screen, 1,300-seat complex offered surround sound in every auditorium and in 1998 was the theater of choice for the first Rehoboth Beach Independent Film Festival, which would return in 1999.

Historic Movie Theaters of Delaware

Trabant University Center Theatre | 1996–present
(Newark)

For all its theater history, Newark is probably best associated with the University of Delaware. Over the years, students from U of D flocked to the town's theaters, so it only made sense that the university should have its own place to screen films—everything from foreign films to recent releases—and at prices college students can afford.

Regal Brandywine Town Center 16 | 1997-Present
(Wilmington)

On the site of the former Brandywine Racetrack was opened the Regal Brandywine Town Center 16, the largest new build the state had/has seen. Like other theaters, the Regal Brandywine was part of a greater shopping center, but this theater offered something no other theater in Delaware could: FunScape.

FunScape was, for all intents and purposes, a miniature indoor theme park located on the ground floor of the ninety-thousand-square-foot facility (the theater itself was on the top floor). FunScape offered laser tag, bumper cars, miniature golf, a go-cart track, a place for little kids to play, party rooms, a mini food court and more. The attractions were separately priced from the theater, but the overall destination made it possible for hours of entertainment, before, after or even in lieu of a movie.

This VIP invitation to FunScape, at the Regal Brandywine Town Center 16, listed every attraction available (except the theater itself). *From the private collection of Rick Roman.*

MOVING PICTURES

Looking to possibly fill the void left by the closure of the State Theatre, the Everett screened a foreign film series across the first three months of 1990, showing one film per month: *Mon Oncle Antoine* (Canada, 1971, set in the French-speaking province of Quebec); Akira Kurosawa's *Dodes'ka-den* (Japan, 1970); and *Shadows of Forgotten Ancestors* (1965) from the Soviet Union. That same year, Movies 6 in Dover became the slightly more corporate Fox Movies 6, while the Midway Palace continued to grow to an at-the-time-largest eight screens.

Older theaters were making news in 1992 and 1993. The Clayton upgraded its sound to a Dolby system, the Everett was being used as a classroom for a Wilmington College course called Aesthetics on Film, and in Dover, there was hope of breathing new life into the long-dormant Capitol Theatre as the Dover Arts Council recognized the city needed a performing arts center. But the cost of using the old Capitol was anywhere from steep ($500,000) to staggering ($2.5 million), so while the desire was there, the time wasn't right. Yet.

Dover's Capitol Theatre, once the Dover Opera House, stood empty and for sale in 1991. *Delaware Public Archives, Dover, Delaware.*

Speaking of new life in old theaters, in the summer of 1995, one of the last drive-in theaters to close in the 1980s, Felton's Diamond State Drive-In, reopened under new manager Donald Brown. Repairs were made, the sound system was upgraded to wireless (540 on the AM dial), vintage twin Peerless Magnarc projectors circa 1940 were installed and when *Die Hard with a Vengeance* rolled on (re)opening night, Delaware was officially removed from the list of four states with no operating drive-ins. The others at the time were Alaska, Rhode Island and New Jersey. New Jersey's place on that list was ironic considering the first drive-in theater in the country opened there in 1933.

In 1998, Richard Derrickson closed the Midway Palace in Rehoboth not just for renovations, but for expansion, and in the process, he raised downstate moviegoing stakes. In 1999, where the Midway Palace once stood, Derrickson opened Movies at Midway, a sixty-one-thousand-square-foot, 2,600-seat, fourteen-screen multiplex. Farther north in Dover, the Carmike Dover (having been acquired from Fox in 1996, along with Fox Movies 6) was ready to make a similar expansion, closing mid-year to be reconfigured from six screens to fourteen. Farther north still, another fundraising effort (the first was in 1996) was underway in Smyrna to restore and reopen the old Opera House.

CLOSING CREDITS

1970–circa 1991: Branmar Cinema | AMC Branmar Twin/2

As the Everett was attempting occasional art house screenings south of Wilmington, Branmar was mixing up its regular programming to include art house films, maybe as a replacement for the closed State Theatre, but definitely as an alternative to art house theaters in Philadelphia. It showed good films, too, including *My Left Foot, Cinema Paradiso* and *The Cook, the Thief, His Wife, and Her Lover*. Ultimately its antiquated equipment and the opening of the new AMC multiplex at Painter's Crossing, just over the Pennsylvania state line (not that far away), was its undoing. It last listed in the spring.

1971–circa 1991: Castle Mall King and Queen | Loews King and Queen

The theater that started the automated projection boom in the state, offering family fare for the first few months before shifting to a schedule that included adult titles, closed quietly in 1991, twenty years after it opened. The last films listed were *Robin Hood: Prince of Thieves* and *Freddy's Dead*.

1972–circa 1992: Triangle Mall Cinema | The Square | Music Makers Theatre | New Castle Square | New Castle Mall | Loew's New Castle Mall | Loew's New Castle Square

The third theater to close in the 1990s was the Loew's New Castle Square. Its last published screenings were *All I Want for Christmas* and *The People Under the Stairs* sharing one screen and *Strictly Business* solo on the other.

1973–1993: Seaford Twin Cinema

The fourth theater to close (and, like the others, a theater with at least twenty years under its belt) was the Seaford Twin. Its last listed screenings were *Trespass* and *A Few Good Men*. "Theater Closed" appeared in listings after that.

1988–1993: BayMart Cinema

About a month before opening his six-screener at the Rehoboth Mall, Richard Derrickson closed his four-screener at BayMart. The woes of the location were evident early.

1973–circa 1996: Chestnut Hill 2 | AMC Chestnut Hill 2 | AMC Chestnut 2 | Chestnut Hill Cinema Café

In February 1993, the AMC Chestnut 2 closed its doors, showing *Sniper* and *Scent of a Woman* as its last films. But they were only the last films of that particular theater's incarnation. In March 1994, Bob Weir, the last owner of the fabled State Theatre, opened the Cinema Café. The concept was simple: show movies, but instead of serving popcorn and soda at a concession stand, have a wait staff serve burgers, fries, nachos, personal pizzas—and beer—to customers. The twenty-one-and-older restaurant/theater hybrid, where the movie tickets were a reasonable $3.50, was a successful model in other parts of the country, so Weir tried it in Delaware. Like it was at the State, Weir's programming here was eclectic. While he predominantly showed recent hits like *Jurassic Park*, he included art house films like *Belle Epoque* and, of course, had Saturday night screenings of *The Rocky Horror Picture Show*. It was a good run, but it came to an end in 1996.

HISTORIC MOVIE THEATERS OF DELAWARE

1969–circa 1998: Dover Cinema | Blue Hen Mall Theater | Blue Hen Mall Concert Hall

The Blue Hen Mall Concert Hall does not appear to have shown movies since it became that entity in 1989, or possibly since 1987, when it changed from Dover Cinema to Blue Hen Mall Theater. It appears to have closed for good in 1998.

1964–1998: Cinema 141 | AMC Cinema 141 | Cinema 141

In February 1993, AMC, citing it had been "out-multiplexed" by new theaters in the area, closed Cinema 141. Two months later, former managers Mike Finocchiaro and Francis Glynn reopened the theater as a discount second-run house. In 1996, they partnered with the Indo-American Association to host a monthly Bollywood film series. A year-long trend of losing money ended that series. On August 3, 1998, using creative scheduling to juggle a five-film day across just two screens—a day that ended with a screening of *Titanic*—Cinema 141 closed for the night. It wouldn't open again, as an overnight fire gutted it.

1970–1999: Concord Mall Cinema | Concord Mall Twin | AMC Concord Mall II/2

When Branmar closed in 1991, people complained to AMC there were no close Delaware venues screening art house films. AMC listened, and with hopes of revitalizing the struggling Concord Mall theater, it introduced art house pictures into its schedule. When the sixteen-screen Regal opened at Town Center (practically around the corner), it was difficult for Concord Mall to be competitive with new releases, so it shifted to art house films exclusively, the only theater in northern Delaware to do so. When the lease was up in 1999, AMC opted not to renew, as twin theaters were too small for its corporate vision. The theater ended its near-thirty-year run with a screening of the Iranian drama *Children of Heaven*.

1970–circa 1999: Tri-State Mall Theater | Eric Tri-State Mall | Cinemagic 5 | Tri-State Theaters

The Tri-State Mall, the state's first-ever multiplex, earned another first in the 1990s—one that wasn't as boastful, though. In 1999, it became the first multiplex with at least five screens to close. Changes began around 1994, when the theater became the Cinemagic 5. By the beginning of 1999, shortly before it appears to have closed, it was a discount theater being managed by Delaware film exhibition veteran Bob Weir.

FADE OUT

The screen-count impact was undeniable in the 1990s, as the five new builds created about fifty new screens in the state. Making certain assumptions, it took about forty-five years for that same number to accumulate beginning in 1868. But that recent growth has proven stable. Of those five new theaters, four are still in operation today, as are theaters that expanded, like the Carmike (now AMC CLASSIC) in Dover and Movies at Midway. And what found itself a thing of the past at the end of the 1990s? The twin theater. Not a single twin existed by 1999.

LOST AND FOUND

Lost theater memories can be found around the state if you know where to look.

This is one of two full-functioning projectors in the Everett Theatre's projection booth. Most film screenings are now digital, but thirty-five millimeter is a viable option there. *Photo by Victoria Nazarewycz.*

TAKE 13
THE NEW MILLENNIUM

Yesterday, Today and Tomorrow

FADE IN

Unlike the decade-driven entries in this book, this chapter will look at 2000–2017 a little differently. First, it will say goodbye to the theaters that closed during the 2000s (Yesterday). Next, it will wrap every theater still open, including those that opened this millennium (Today). Finally, there will be a few notes about theatrical goings-on that could shape the future (Tomorrow).

YESTERDAY

With the permanent closure of only six theaters (including the Shalimar, which was covered in Seeking Stardom in the 1950s), the new millennium is the most stable period in the state's history. Sure, there were only six closures from 1900 to 1909 and only five from 1940 to 1949, but those occurred in almost half the time as the 2000s, giving the 2000s a better closures-per-year rate.

1981–circa 2000: Movies 6 | Fox Movies 6 | Carmike Movies 6

In 2000, Carmike Cinemas Inc. filed for bankruptcy protection. Part of its strategy to restructure was to close smaller, sometimes older, unprofitable (or less profitable) theaters and keep newer, better-performing places open. Movies 6 fit all three negative descriptions—small, old, poor-performing—and faced competition with its more attractive corporate sibling, the fourteen-screener at the Dover Mall.

1979–2002: Christiana Mall Cinema | AMC Christiana Mall

Early in this book I talk about theaters and theatrical entities, and of all the decisions I made on how to group theaters, this was the toughest call. The Christiana Mall Cinema, later called the AMC Christiana Mall, closed its doors in 2002, another victim of lean financial times and the desire of theatrical corporations to focus their resources on newer, fancier places. When the theater closed, the mall opted to not pursue another theater to take its place and instead converted that space into retail stores. This is the main reason why I chose to keep this entity separate from the new theater now at the mall: there was never intent to replace the original theater. When the new theater opened in 2014, it was done so as an independent action and wholly removed from the original theater (by a different company, in a different decade, at a different location detached from the mall).

1993–2008: Rehoboth Mall Cinema

After hosting the Rehoboth Beach Independent Film Festival into the early 2000s, the otherwise little-covered Rehoboth Mall Cinema, which had become a second-run theater, closed unexpectedly in October 2008, citing mounting debt to the mall against poor attendance and deteriorating conditions.

1949–2008: Diamond State Drive-In | Hiway 13 Drive-In | Diamond State Drive-In

In 1995, the Diamond State Drive-In rose like a phoenix from the ashes of the past. In 2008, Delaware's reborn open-air theater returned to the ashes from which it came. The Steele family, owners of the property the theater was leasing, decided not to renew that lease. On Saturday, November 29, after a family-friendly double feature of *Bolt* and *Madagascar: Escape 2 Africa*, the theater closed for good.

1870–2017: Dover Opera House/Nixon's Opera House/New Dover Opera House | Capital/Capitol Theatre | Schwartz Center for the Arts

Having been closed since 1982, and having flirted with comebacks, the Capitol Theatre was finally resurrected in October 2001 with a $7.8 million restoration and an opening night concert by country legend Rosanne Cash. The theater's new name was homage to the family synonymous with the Dover theater scene: Schwartz Center for the Arts. Five days after that gala open, the theater would host the world premiere screening of the documentary *Whispers of Angels: A Story of the Underground Railroad*. After a decade and a half providing live performances and film screenings, the Schwartz Center closed in 2017, the victim of lagging revenue, the loss of two major contributors (representing one-sixth of its budget) and the reduction in government arts funding.

TODAY

Overall, of the 150 theaters I found in my research, across a timeline that spans 150 years, 22 theaters in total are open as of this writing. Of them, 18 still show movies with some kind of regularity, 14 of which are full-time movie theaters, with a total screen count of 123.

Cinema Art Theater | 17701 Dartmouth Drive, Lewes | since 2016

In 2016, the beaches had a new single-screen theater for the first time in decades: Lewes' Cinema Art Theater. The 108-seat venue, built by the Rehoboth Beach Film Society, is open year-round, specializes in independent films and serves as a location for screenings during the society's annual film festival.

The view from the back row of the cozy Cinema Art Theater, the most recent new theater established in Delaware (as of this writing). *Photo by Victoria Nazarewycz.*

Cinemark Christiana and XD | 1200 Mall Road, Newark | since 2014

After the AMC Christiana Mall closed its doors in 2002, the mall would go without a theater until 2014 when Cinemark, already with ten screens in its older Wilmington theater, opened a standalone building in a large area mostly surrounded by parking. Cinemark introduced the state's third premium large-format screen (like IMAX, but not that brand; it is known as XD), and when it saw the shift to recliners in other multiplexes, it followed suit.

Westown Movies | 150 Commerce Drive, Middletown | since 2013

The new millennium saw considerable population growth in the Middletown, Odessa and Townsend (MOT) area, and with it came a boom of eateries, retailers and a new multiplex. Westown Movies, a theater with all the comforts of a modern theater, is also one in touch with the roots of Middletown's history. The lobby's sweeping mural is an homage to Middletown past and present, including a prominent image of the Everett Theatre. It has given back to the community by allowing a local church to hold services there each Sunday, it features edibles made by local establishments, and from 2015 through 2017, the theater allowed the MOT Film Society to present classic films on select Sundays to raise money for local and regional charities. The theater was the second in the state to offer a premium large-format experience (what it calls GTX) with a state-of-the-art Dolby Atmos sound system.

Also part of the theater's young legacy is how it successfully lobbied to allow alcohol to be sold in movie theaters in the state. Delaware, true to some of its roots when it comes to "sinful" things, had a ban on alcohol sales in movie theaters. Westown got that changed, and it wasn't long before other multiplexes offered adult beverages.

Penn Cinema Riverfront & IMAX | 401 South Madison Street, Wilmington | since 2012

Penn Cinema Riverfront & IMAX opened in December 2012, and when it did, it laid claim to a pair of consequential firsts. At fifteen screens, it was the first multiplex inside city limits. For all of Wilmington's rich theatrical history (it's been home to about one-third of the state's theaters ever), only five had more than one screen, and four of those were in the suburbs; Penn was the fifth. Another first for the theater: it was the first, and is still the only, genuine IMAX theater in Delaware. And in its short tenure, the theater has already seen a major change—most of its auditoriums' seats have been converted to recliners.

Theatre N at Nemours | 1007 North Orange Street, Wilmington | since 2002

For the first time in twenty years, a dedicated movie theater was flickering inside city limits. Operated by the city's Cultural Affairs Office, Theatre N at Nemours debuted on October 4 with *Sunshine State*, a fine example of the indie fare it planned to specialize in. The theater, the first new place to open in the state in the new millennium, did well early, even though it was only open on weekends. It would soon take part in, or host, events like the Wilmington Independent Film Festival, the Beth Shalom Winter Film Series and the OUTflix Film Festival.

In the theater's later years, the city struggled to properly manage the place; complaints ranged from website issues to the theater being closed when it was scheduled to show films. In 2016, it was shuttered without warning but would soon reopen under private management. Now, the theater, whose dedicated team of four includes Delaware theater veteran Bob Weir (as technical director), still specializes in independent films, offers both digital and thirty-five-millimeter projections and hosts other events like televised football games, operas, ballets and even the occasional *Rocky Horror* screening.

Regal Brandywine Town Center 16 | 3300 Brandywine Parkway, Wilmington | since 1997

The Regal Brandywine went through a major change in 2000. Regal Cinemas, at the time the nation's largest exhibitor, was having financial trouble, so it closed the FunScape portion of those theaters that had it, including Brandywine. While the go-cart track is long gone, you still need to take a pair of escalators to get to the top-floor theater, which has since been remodeled. All sixteen screens now have reserved recliner seating.

Trabant University Center Theatre | 17 West Main Street, Newark | since 1996

The Trabant University Center Theatre continues to offer first- and second-run films for University of Delaware students (and still at student-friendly prices).

Regal Peoples Plaza Stadium 17 | 1100 Peoples Plaza, Newark | since 1992

The landscape of the shopping center known as Peoples Plaza has changed over time, but the Regal itself has remained a strong constant, screening Hollywood hits, some smaller films and offerings from Bollywood. To this day, this remains the theater with the most screens in the state's history.

Recently, like its sister theater in Brandywine, this stadium converted to all-reserved, all-reclining seats.

Cinemark Movies 10 | 1796 West Newport Pike, Wilmington | since 1991

At one time the biggest multiplex in the state, Movies 10 is now one of the oldest multiplexes in the state, and it is certainly the oldest multiplex never to have expanded beyond its original screen count.

Riverfront Theater | 2 South Walnut Street, Milford | since 1989

In 2015, the Second Street Players at the Riverfront Theater provided something to Milford the town hadn't had since 1983: a movie theater. After a grant afforded the chance to purchase projection equipment and a screen, the "Movies @ Riverfront Theater" (MaRT) program kicked off its monthly five-dollar screenings with *The Avengers* (2012). Embracing a model of old, the Riverfront began as a live theater and has since incorporated movies to offer a wider variety of entertainment to its community.

AMC CLASSIC Dover 14 | 1365 North DuPont Highway, Dover | since 1983

This multiplex inside the Dover Mall has been a mainstay in the state capital for more than three decades. In 2017, AMC took over Carmike, changing the theater's corporate brand. At one point in time, Dover had five different public movie theaters in simultaneous existence. Today, the Dover 14 stands as the only full-time public movie theater in all of Kent County.

Movies at Midway | 18585 Coastal Highway, Rehoboth Beach | since 1965

In a move I believe to be the first in the state's history (and if not, certainly the first in the state's history with a theater of this size), Midway actually decreased its number of screens by one. In late 2017, the theater closed

On the left is one of the thirty-five-millimeter projectors at Movies at Midway. On the right is one of the theater's set of platters. Platters are used to spool multiple film reels together into one large film reel so a projectionist does not have to manually switch reels of film during a show. (This is especially helpful when there are fourteen screens.) The theater has since converted its daily projection to digital. *Photo by Victoria Nazarewycz.*

two of its auditoriums and combined them into one large screening room, dubbing it "The Cube." The Cube is the state's fourth, and latest, premium large-format venue, and it has a Dolby Atmos sound system. At thirteen screens, Midway is Sussex County's largest theater and within the top five in the state.

Main Street Movies 5 | 230 East Main Street, Newark | since 1963

No sooner were we in the new millennium than the Cinema Center announced its closure. Owned by AMC, the company did not renew its lease and continued its focus on newer, bigger theaters. The closure didn't last long. Mike Finacchiaro and Francis Glynn, former owners of Cinema 141, bought the place, reserving one screen for art house fare and the other two for second-run movies. They even picked up the *Rocky Horror* mantle.

Time caught up with the old place, and with a slowdown in business and mounting debt, the theater closed in 2015. But as has been the case with many theaters in Delaware's history, it wasn't gone for long, although its return took another form. In 2017, after a multimillion-dollar renovation, the Cinema Center was reborn and the three-screener was now a five: Main Street Movies 5, a theater with all modern amenities, including reserved recliner seating, beer and wine sales, electronic ticketing and (some) food supplied by Newark pizzerias and bakeries.

Like Westown, Main Street respects history. In its lobby hangs one of the original Cinema Center signs.

Clayton Theatre | 33246 Main Street, Dagsboro | since 1949

In 2013, the Clayton Theatre faced a crisis. Hollywood was moving away from thirty-five-millimeter and running toward digital. But with this shift—yet another tech advance in a long history of tech advances—the Clayton faced an uncertain future. The community rallied behind the theater it grew up with by attending fundraising screenings, supporting partnerships with other merchants and even writing a book presenting something of an oral history of the theater, all to raise the $85,000 needed for the upgrade to digital projection in 2014. The Clayton still has its two thirty-five-millimeter projectors, although one is now for display purposes only. The other projector functions, and on those occasions when it rolls thirty-five-millimeter, there is an intermission during the reel change. Keeping true to its roots, the Clayton offers classic film screenings on select Mondays, and the balcony is always open for seating.

The Theater at Dover Air Force Base | Dover Air Force Base, Dover | since circa 1941

As it has from its inception, the theater at the Dover Air Force Base, now managed by AAFES Reel Time Theatres, continues to provide first-run features to those stationed there. In 2013, the base upgraded its projector from thirty-five-millimeter to digital.

Historic Movie Theaters of Delaware

Candlelight Theatre | 2208 Millers Road, Wilmington | since 1931

In 2004, the Candlelight Music Dinner Theatre changed its name to the New Candlelight Theatre, and ten years later, it dropped "New" and became the Candlelight Theatre, a live entertainment and dining venue.

Milton Theatre | 110 Union Street, Milton | since 1919

Three decades after its closing, the Milton Theatre began a restoration project in 2000 and reopened in 2003 as a live theater, but it also screened movies. The recession of the late 2000s put another end to the theater, as it closed its doors in 2010 after a fundraising screening of *Rocky Horror*. But it wasn't done yet. In 2013, the theater came back to life, again with live shows. It is very active today, and live music, comedy and other performances aren't all it offers. Once a month, Revival House, self-described as "A Religious Experience for Film Lovers," screens movies rep-house style, with an eclectic mix of cult faves, rockin' docs and even the chance for local filmmakers to showcase their work.

The Queen Wilmington | 500 North Market Street, Wilmington | since 1916

The former Market Street movie house known as the Queen remained dormant from 1959 until 2011, when, after a $25 million overhaul, it reopened as a live music venue (an extension of Philadelphia's World Café Live). In 2017, Live Nation assumed management control.

Playhouse on Rodney Square | 1007 North Market Street, Wilmington | since 1913

The Playhouse changed its name to the DuPont Theatre in 2003, then to the Playhouse on Rodney Square in 2015. As it has been for decades, the Playhouse's specialty is Broadway fare, offering productions of everything from *Les Misérables* to *Jersey Boys*. It may have flirted with film early in its one-hundred-plus-year history, but it has always been in love with live theater and still is to this day.

Historic Movie Theaters of Delaware

The Grand | 818 North Market Street, Wilmington | since 1871

With a focus on live events, the Grand expanded its brand in 2000 by acquiring the lots next door (home of the once mighty Aldine) and opening the Baby Grand. It also assumed management of the Playhouse on Rodney Square in 2015. The Grand presents more than eighty live shows per season, including performances by the Delaware Symphony, Opera Delaware and First State Ballet.

Smyrna Opera House | 7 West South Street, Smyrna | since 1870

After being closed for about fifty-five years, the last four of which were spent renovating, the Smyrna Opera House reopened its refurbished doors to the public in 2003. Its ground floor remained the library it had become, but the auditorium itself was fully restored on the second floor, including a balcony above. Part of Smyrna's opening program included an appearance by Frederick Douglass IV, the great-grandson of Frederick Douglass, who had spoken at the Opera House soon after its 1870 open. The Smyrna Opera House was designed to offer both film and live presentations; the latter is its main attraction.

Everett Theatre | 51 West Main Street, Middletown | since 1868

Finally, and again, the place where it all began.

Over the course of the 2000s, the Everett Theatre has continued to be the hub of arts in MOT, with year-round programming consisting of both live productions and film (including annual participation in the Manhattan Short Film Festival). This hasn't happened without challenges.

In March 2008, hours after 150 patrons left a live Easter production, an eighty-five-by-sixty-foot chunk of ceiling collapsed in the seating area, forcing the theater to close and creating a need for $500,000 in renovations and upgrades (of which insurance covered about half). It was a tall order, but this was the Everett Theatre, a venue that had already bounced back from two fires (as the Middletown Opera House) and two business-related closures. A fundraising campaign helped get the theater where it needed to be, and in May 2009, the Everett reopened.

In addition to fires and finances and falling ceilings, the Everett had one other hurdle to clear: a foe. In its history, the Everett faced almost no local competition, but in 2013, Westown Movies opened less than two miles away. Because of the rules of film distribution, the new twelve-screen first-run theater changed the dynamic of what films the Everett could show and when, impacting its screening schedule. The oldest theatrical entity in the state's history adapted and placed a greater emphasis on live shows but also upgraded its projection system to digital to stay competitive and to meet the demands of Hollywood (although its twin Peerless projectors still work just fine).

As of late, the theater's film focus has been to partner with local charities to show fundraising family films.

TOMORROW

It's impossible to know what fate 2018 and beyond holds, but given how many theaters in Delaware have come back from the dead, it wouldn't surprise me if others did. In fact, two theaters are trying to do just that.

In Millsboro, Eric Clarke and his wife, Dr. Julie Hattier, purchased the building that housed the Ball Theatre (which was mostly preserved inside) and are slowly renovating it to a venue for films and live events. Also looking to reopen is the recently closed Schwartz Center for the Arts. Community members are organizing to understand how it got into the trouble it did and how to reopen the place.

In new theater news, Arthur Helmick, who has been involved in the creation of Westown Movies and the resurrection of the Cinema Center in the form of Main Street Movies 5, is looking to open his third Delaware theater by the summer of 2019 in Milford. To be located in the old Walmart building on U.S. 113, the nine-screen Milford Movies will be Delaware's first theater equipped with laser projectors.

While two theaters look to revive history and a third theater looks to make new history, a fourth theater is having its history solidified. Slated to receive a formal historical marker from the Delaware Archives is the Milton Theatre. (On a personal note, I had the great privilege to contribute historical information and text for that marker.)

FADE OUT

Since the 1980s, movie-watching has made a steady migration away from theaters and into the home. From cable movie channels and **VHS** to streaming movie channels and **VOD**, the entertainment industry has been luring movie lovers to stay home, where it's more comfortable and much cheaper. While home video isn't the sole reason for the shrinking number of movie theaters, it certainly is a factor. But what makes this problem unique is that the problem can be solved by you.

Go to the movies tomorrow. Support your local theater tomorrow, whether it has one screen or seventeen. Pay the experience forward tomorrow to the younger people in your life and take them to the movies. Watching a movie in a theater can come with challenges, but there is nothing like sharing the experience of film with a room full of strangers. I've seen enough movies first at the theater then later at home (and vice versa) to know every experience in the theater is a different one than the one at home. You control their fates. Keep theaters alive.

— FADE TO BLACK —

ROLL CREDITS

From theater owners to concession stand attendees, the number of people who have played a part in the history of Delaware movie theaters is impossible to know. However, there were and are individuals whose contributions have gone beyond the day-to-day business of theaters. You've seen some of their names throughout this book. Here is a little about them.

PIONEERS

WILLIAM DOCKSTADER
In a state full of firsts, William Dockstader could be considered Delaware's First Movie Man. Born in the Frankford section of Philadelphia in 1852, Dockstader's early attempts at a career in showbiz failed, and his parents wanted him to quit. Instead, he set out with stock vaudeville companies, traveling the country until he came back east and started a troupe of his own. He had a knack for management, and in the early 1890s, against the advice of friends, he moved to Wilmington, where he opened the Wilmington Musee, where he eventually showed *The Kiss*, and went on to launch the Garrick, where he screened *The Great Train Robbery*.

W.O. Hyrup

If the people couldn't get to moving pictures, W.O. Hyrup got moving pictures to the people. In the heart of the first decade of the twentieth century, Hyrup routinely took screenings on the road. Those screenings would be held at several places found in this book, including the Academy of Music (as the Avenue), the New Castle Opera House, Shellpot and Brandywine Springs Parks and the Grand. He also screened moving pictures in various halls, and when an occasion happened outdoors, Hyrup happened with it, at one time showing films at a street carnival.

Charles Topkis and James N. Ginns

The partners of Topkis-Ginns were once the theater kings of Wilmington's Market Street. In the 1920s, the duo owned, leased or managed some of the most storied theaters on the city's main thoroughfare: the Aldine, Arcadia, Garrick, Majestic and Rialto. They also owned two theaters that are still with us today: Market Street's Queen and Playhouse. The pairing also has a unique connection to theater history before and after them. In the before column, they acquired the Garrick from original owner (and fellow pioneer) William Dockstader. In the after column, Ginns had a daughter named Reba who went on to marry George M. Schwartz (of Dover theater fame) and, with her stepdaughter Muriel, successfully ran the Schwartz theater business for decades after George passed.

LEGACIES

Of the 150 theaters in this book, 134 span between 1917 and today. Of those 134 theaters, nearly 20 percent were owned by just three families, and during that time, at least one of those families has always owned at least one theater.

The Schwartz Family

In 1917, George Schwartz began a theatrical empire that started with the Temple Theatre and went on to include Dover's Capitol, Smyrna's Strand and Middletown's Everett. After he passed in 1942, his wife, Reba, and daughter Muriel took over the business, expanding both south to Sussex County (the second Delmar Drive-In), farther north into New Castle County

(Cinema Center and Branmar) and in their home base of Kent County with the Dover Cinema, Kent Drive-In and Towne. The family stayed in the business until 1979.

The Ayers Family

Thomas Ayers, born in New Jersey and sent to a Georgetown, Delaware foster home because his parents were too poor to raise him, worked hard in his youth, an ethic that paid off when, in 1933, he purchased Seaford's Palace Theatre and Georgetown's Sussex Theatre. Ayers would go on to build two new theaters: the Layton in Seaford and the Sidney in Bridgeville. It was during the Sidney build in 1948 that Ayers suffered a heart attack and was forced to retire from the exhibition business. In stepped his son, nineteen-year-old Layton, to assume the leadership reins. The family movie business, which at one point grew its own corn for popping, went on to last until 1984.

The Derrickson Family

Between Milford native William Derrickson, his son Richard and Richard's daughter Tiffany, the Derricksons might be better categorized as Delaware's Movie Theater Dynasty. What started at the beach in 1941 has become a legacy of single-screeners, drive-ins, mall denizens and state-of-the-art multiplexes, most of which have called Rehoboth home. Father and son Derrickson built, rebuilt or at one time owned twelve theaters between 1941 and now: the Avenue, Center, Beachwood and Rehoboth Twin theaters on Rehoboth Avenue; the BayMart and Rehoboth Mall Cinemas in the greater Rehoboth area; the Midway, Sussex West and Twin Oaks drive-ins; the Layton and the Clayton around Sussex County; and finally the Movies at Midway (formerly the Midway Palace), the only theater among the three families to be owned and operated by the same family and remain open today. Tiffany Derrickson, the only third-generation theater person in the state, is co-owner of the Midway today (with her father), and rather than rest on the laurels of being the sole multiplex south of Dover, she recognizes the past as it fits within the construct of the future, having added the only premium large-format screening room south of Middletown. In addition to that, she programs an excellent blend of Hollywood blockbusters and mainstream indies.

LEADING LADIES

IDA FOX

Ida Fox became one of the first women managers of a Delaware movie theater when her son, William, passed away unexpectedly in 1919. (That said, she was responsible for opening the theater for him in the first place.) In 1920, she became the first woman in the state to register to vote, and in 1923, when she was the only woman manager in the state, she declined consideration to be Milton's mayor, as she had too many business interests to focus on.

Frances Merchant

In 1936, Wilmington's *News Journal* formally announced its first-ever film critic, Frances Merchant, whose Cinema Slants column became Views and Previews. The first film she reviewed was *One Rainy Afternoon*, starring Ida Lupino and produced by Mary Pickford. Merchant liked it but seemed unimpressed by Lupino.

HELEN E. TINDALL

After years of working in various capacities at Wilmington's Warner theaters, and eventually as assistant manager at the Ritz, Tindall found herself thrust into the position of running the Ritz in the absence of her manager in 1943. Her lead management role was a first for a woman in Wilmington, after being the first female assistant manager in the city. During her tenure as manager, she became involved in the city theaters' March of Dimes campaigns.

JOANNE HOWE

The owner of the Clayton Theatre since 2000, Joanne Howe understands history. While first-run films keep the lights on at Delaware's only public single-screen theater to run Hollywood's newest mainstream fare, history is embraced both on-screen and in-theater. On many Monday nights, the Clayton presents classic films, with trivia-filled introductions and a glorious view from the balcony (to which I can personally attest, having screened *The Bishop's Wife* there—for research, of course). The theater is a living time machine, with its external box office, its simple but satisfying concession stand and the endless bits of nostalgia on display throughout.

LEADING MEN

A. Joseph DeFiore

It may have been in Philadelphia where Naples, Italy native A.J. DeFiore got his start in the theater business, but it was in Wilmington where he made his mark, first as manager of the Broadway Theatre (originally the Victory Theatre), then later in the same capacity at the Park Theatre on Union Street. For thirty years, DeFiore knew nothing but service. At his theaters, he was forever committed to improving exhibition. In his industry, he served as president of the Motion Picture Theater Owners of Delaware, vice chairman of the War Activities Committee war bond drive, state chairman of the War Activities Committee Red Cross drive, member of the National Committee for the Motion Picture Industry to assist with WAC recruiting, state March of Dimes chairman (a position that earned him several invitations to the White House) and other titles. And in his community he was a respected civic leader, heavily involved in local politics and chairman of the Italian CARE group, a program that shipped morale-building care packages to members of Italian non-Communist parties.

Lewis Black

While A.J. DeFiore eventually made it *to* Wilmington before making it *in* Wilmington, another of the city's theater-managing titans, Lewis Black, was *from* Wilmington and made it *in* his hometown. Black's career in movies began as an employee of Warner—not the theater, but the company that owned the Garrick, Aldine, Arcadia and Queen, all for which Black managed publicity and promotion. But it was when he was charged with managing the new Warner Theatre, and months later appointed city manager for all of Wilmington's Warner-owned theaters, that Black's star rocketed. The only manager the Warner ever knew from its 1939 opening to its 1973 sale was an industry celebrity, with responsibilities that included president of the Theatre Managers' Club of Wilmington and president of the Wilmington Theatre Managers Association. In the community, he was a pillar, serving as chairman of the Merchants Committee and acting as a member of the Chamber of Commerce Managing Committee, Delaware Safety Council, Red Cross Public Information Committee and Handicapped Advisory Committee. He also participated in the March of Dimes and was a member of the mayor's Civilian Military Affairs Committee.

That last item was in 1951, and Black surely earned that position thanks to the staggering work he did in support of World War II. Over those several years, Black was chief deputy air raid warden for movie houses, a defense bond motion picture representative, New Castle County chair for the Army and Navy Emergency Relief Fund, chairman of the State War Bond Committee, chairman of the War Activities Committee, chairman of that infamous Fifth War Loan Bond Drive and responsible for all motion picture promotion as part of the War Advertising and Publicity Committee.

Black may not have gone "over there," but the impact of the work he did right here was immeasurable. Lewis Black died in 2001 at the age of ninety-five.

REESE HARRINGTON

A theater man from the time he was a boy (he operated silent pictures in the Reese Opera House at age eleven), Reese Harrington came into his own when his Reese Theatre became the first theater south of Wilmington to screen a sound picture; he considered the moment to be inferior. Truthfully, he considered the quality of the sound to be inferior—so much so he held off on upgrading his place until he visited thirty-two regional theaters to perform a comparison of sound systems. This keen sense for technology would become a Reese Harrington trademark, as he forever tinkered with or overhauled his theaters' audio and visual technology to provide the best moviegoing experience his audience could have. Add to that his work with the Central Committee of the Community of Friendly Neighbors, and Harrington would not only fit in with exhibitors of today, he'd also be leading the way to make exhibition better.

CHARLES S. HORN AND BARRY SOLAN

Two theater owners separated by decades and by the better part of the length of the state share a unique connection. Horn, as owner of the Blue Hen in Rehoboth in 1939, took on blue laws, which told people *when* they were prohibited from watching movies at their local theater. Solan, as owner of the State in Newark in 1982, took on adult entertainment licensing, which told people *which* movies they were prohibited from watching at their local theater. Both men, whose ownership timelines didn't overlap but whose life timelines did (Solan was born in the early 1950s, Horn passed away in the mid-1970s), recognized the importance of giving people the full experience of when, where and which movies they wanted to see, not when/where/which movies as dictated by the government. In both cases, the men's actions affected laws for the betterment of moviegoers.

Bob Weir

Along the latter portion of Delaware's movie theater timeline, one name stands out: Bob Weir. Weir has spent decades dedicated to providing great theater experiences for Delaware's film fanatics. Perhaps his inspiration was born at the age of seven, when he got a glimpse inside the projection booth at the Pleasant Hill Drive-In and saw what he describes as "the sun in a box." Starting as a projectionist at the State (where the first film he projected was *The Rocky Horror Picture Show*, a film he has since projected over 1,700 times), Weir went on to reopen that place, launch the Cinema Café and run the theater at the Tri-State Mall.

In between and since, Weir has played roles at the Christiana, Triangle and Castle Malls; the Grand, the Playhouse and the Schwartz Center; the Rialto; and the Trabant at the U of D. And his multifaceted relationship with the Everett includes having served on the board, worked as a projectionist, hosted his own film screenings (including *It's a Wonderful Life*) and served as a grip on the *Dead Poets Society* shoot (adjacent to which was his projection work at the Museum of Natural History when it held its charity screening of that film).

Today, Weir serves as technical director at Wilmington's Theatre N and, in a move reminiscent of W.O. Hyrup, has held numerous outdoor screenings all over the state, showing them on the current trend: an inflatable screen. Whether serving up beer and blockbusters for dinner, *Rocky Horror* treats at midnight or things more discriminating in between, Weir has been the Renaissance man Delaware movie fans have needed.

Richard Roman

Despite operating from his native Ohio, Richard Roman has been a key part of four important theaters in Delaware. His first foray into the First State began when he was an independent consultant working for Regal Theaters in the 1990s, when he helped broker the deal to place the theater in Peoples Plaza. Later, while helping Regal expand, he pitched an idea that went on to become the groundbreaking FunScape. Fast-forward to 2013, and Roman, under his Roman Theatre Management banner, oversaw the creation of

Westown Movies in Middletown, the town where movie theaters began. And in 2017, he was key in the resurrection of Newark's historic Cinema Center in its new form as Main Street Movies 5.

SUPPORTING CAST

Somewhere between movie theater people and movie theater patrons are the groups that champion both. Clubs, committees and societies formed for the betterment of motion picture exhibition and the moviegoing experience have been around almost as long as motion picture exhibition and the moviegoing experience. Here are those I found in my travels through history.

Motion Pictures Committee of the Delaware State Federation of Women's Clubs

The earliest reference I found on this committee was in 1928, although the overall federation formed in 1899. The responsibilities taken on by the committee (at least through 1944) included working with theaters to provide film screenings for children and to provide higher quality films for the community at large. For its members, the committee offered film studies and published previews of films that would appear at Wilmington theaters.

Kent County Better Films Council and Wilmington Better Films Council

Appearing in the early 1930s and working toward the greater common interest of their respective communities, the Kent County and Wilmington Better Films Councils were parts of a national organization whose primary interest was ensuring (morally) better films were made available to the public. The groups also addressed larger issues, including an opposition to block booking, interest in film- and theater-related legislation and one 1941 topic, motion pictures in national defense.

Brandywine Film Society

In 1966, a grass-roots organization thought it would be a good thing to make available to the public films of "artistic and cultural merit." The Brandywine Film Society kicked off a nine-film series in September that year; membership to see all nine films was eight dollars. The films that inaugural season, which screened in the Tower Hill School auditorium, included *Grand Hotel* and *To Have and Have Not*. The Brandywine Film Society carried this tradition at least through 1973.

Cultural Center Cinema Committee and Wilmington Cinema Committee

A pair of film appreciation organizations were founded in Wilmington in 1967, and it's no surprise they were confused with each other. One was the Cultural Center Cinema Committee (affiliated with the Wilmington Cultural Center). The other was the Wilmington Cinema Committee. Both groups specialized in films not found in theaters; the CCCC's specialty was experimental films and the WCC's was foreign films, and they occasionally drifted into each other's lanes. Ultimately, viewer interest was not there for either group, and both folded in 1971.

Newark Film Revival Society

No organization committed to film is too small for this book. Neal Van Duren's Newark Film Revival Society, with news entries found only in 1980, screened a collection of comedy shorts at the State Theatre that year, including works from the Marx Brothers, W.C. Fields, Laurel & Hardy and Looney Tunes.

Rehoboth Beach Film Society

In the fall of 1997, five Rehoboth Beach film lovers got together to consider the possibility of showing independent films in local restaurants. By the fall of 1998, their ranks had grown, the Rehoboth Beach Film Society had been formally founded, it became a not-for-profit and it hosted the first Rehoboth Beach Independent Film Festival. When it left its six-screen residence at the Rehoboth Mall in the early 2000s, it didn't go far, landing up the road at the fourteen-screen Movies at Midway, where it continued annually through 2014. The festival has become *the* annual film-related event in the state, and when the society was challenged with finding screening locations, it rose to that challenge and opened its own venue, the Cinema Art Theater.

HISTORIC MOVIE THEATERS OF DELAWARE

MOT FILM SOCIETY

From his kitchen table in December 2014, the author started the MOT Film Society with the goal of bringing classic movies to the big screens of MOT's newest and oldest theaters: Westown and the Everett. At the Everett, the society screened classics like *Casablanca*, *The Searchers*, *Mister Roberts* and *Yankee Doodle Dandy*. At Westown, the society helped raise thousands of dollars for local and regional charities over the course of three years and almost fifty screenings, with titles ranging from *Gone with the Wind* and *The Wizard of Oz* to *The Goonies* and *Jurassic Park*. The society also hosted its own film festival at Westown in 2015. The Directed by Women Film Festival was a three-day, ten-film screening and celebration of films directed by women. Titles screened included Oscar winners (Kathryn Bigelow's *The Hurt Locker*), blockbusters (Nora Ephron's *Sleepless in Seattle*), classics (Ida Lupino's *The Hitch-Hiker*) and indies (Joyce Wu's *She Lights Up Well*).

The author founded the MOT Film Society in December 2014. *Logo design by Victoria Nazarewycz.*

SOURCES

Newspapers

Baltimore Sun
Cape Gazette
Daily Gazette (Wilmington, DE)
Daily Republican (Wilmington, DE)
Daily Times (Salisbury, MD)
Delawarean
Delaware Pilot
Delaware State News
Delaware Wave
Delmarva News
Denton (MD) Journal
Dialog
Dover Post
Evening Journal (Wilmington, DE)
Evening Times (Cumberland, MD)
Middletown Transcript
Milford Beacon
Milford Chronicle
Morning News (Wilmington, DE)
Newark Post
New Castle Gazette
New Castle Weekly
News Journal (Wilmington, DE)
Philadelphia Inquirer
Philadelphia Times
Star-Democrat (Easton, MD)
Sun (Wilmington, DE)

Publications

Arat, Joanna L. *DuPont Theatre*. Charleston, SC: Arcadia Publishing, 2012.
Blagg, G. Daniel. *Dover: A Pictorial History*. Virginia Beach, VA: Donning Company Publishers, 1980.
Cahn, Julius. *Julius Cahn's Official Theatrical Guide*. Vols. 1–16, 20. Self-published, 1896–1913, 1921.

Federal Writers' Project. *Delaware: A Guide to the First State*. New York: Viking, 1938.
Francis, William. *Along the Christina River*. Charleston, SC: Arcadia Publishing, 2013.
Franklin, Albert. *Memories of Frankford*. Self-published, 2003.
Gerken, Sandie Hancock. *Memories of the Clayton Theatre: A Look Back*. Self-published, 2013.
Greenwood Bicentennial Committee. *Greenwood: A Delaware Town*. Self-published, 1976.
Grunder, Betty. "Up in Smoke." *Journal of the Lewes Historical Society* 11 (November 2008).
Lawlor, Mark R. *Brandywine Springs Amusement Park: Echoes of the Past 1886–1923*. Wilmington, DE: M&M Publishing, 1991.
Maynard, W. Barksdale. *Buildings of Delaware*. Charlottesville: University of Virginia Press, 2008.
McNinch, Marjorie. *The Silver Screen*. Wilmington, DE: Cedar Tree Books, Ltd., 1997.
McVey, Shauna. *Middletown*. Charleston, SC: Arcadia Publishing, 2014.
Messick, Kendall. *The Projectionist*. New York: Princeton Architectural Press, 2010.
Newark Planning Department. *Historic Buildings of Newark, Delaware*. Self-published, 1983.
Scharf, J. Thomas. *History of Delaware*. Vol. 2. Philadelphia: J.L. Richard & Company, 1888.
Schiek, Martha. *Claymont*. Charleston, SC: Arcadia Publishing, 2000.
Sparks, John N., Jr. *History of Union Lodge #5 A.F. & A.M.* Self-published, 1986.
Staff. "Drivin' 'Round the Drive-Ins." *The Billboard*, June 19, 1954.
Willey, Shannon. *Seaford, Delaware*. Charleston, SC: Arcadia Publishing, 1999.
Young, Toni. *The Grand Experience: A Drama in Five Acts, Containing a Description of Wilmington's Grand Opera House & Masonic Temple, a Victorian Building in the Second Empire Style, and a History of the Many Parts It Has Played in the Delaware Community for More than a Century*. Wilmington, DE: American Life Foundation for the Grand Opera House, 1976.

Sources

Websites

atlasobscura.com
candlelighttheatredelaware.com
chroniclingamerica.loc.gov
cinematour.com
cinematreasures.org
deadmalls.com
delawareonline.com
delawarescene.com
delawarestatenews.net
delcode.delaware.gov
delmardustpan.blogspot.com
delmarhistoricalandartsociety.
 blogspot.com
delmarvanow.com
dover.af.mil
dpr.delaware.gov
drive-ins.com
driveins.org
driveintheater.com
dsdit.com
duponttheatre.com
everetttheatre.com
fortdupont.org
fortmilesha.org
fortwiki.com
imdbpro.com
loc.gov
middletownde.org
milfordlive.com
militaryheritage.org
newrivernotes.com
newspapers.com
newsworks.org
nc-chap.org
oakknollbooks.wordpress.com
ocmuseum.org
oldwilmington.net
paintedstave.com
queen.worldcafelive.com
rehobothfilm.com
revivalhousetheater.com
schwartzcenter.com
secondstreetplayers.com
smyrnaoperahouse.org
tcm.com
theatren.com
theclaytontheatre.com
thegrandwilmington.org
udel.edu
uxoinfo.com
variety.com
wboc.com

ABOUT THE AUTHOR

Michael's youth was spent during the era he considers the Golden Age of Film Fandom: 1974 to 1989, when drive-ins, single-screeners and multiplexes were simultaneously popular; when broadcast networks and UHF stations offered steady diets of everything from classics to blockbusters to late-night schlock; and when premium cable and home video exploded with twenty-four-hour film programming. For all the movies he's seen in that time and since, he has only two regrets: missing the triple feature that closed the 1986 season at Naamans Drive-In and not saving the old *Halliwell's Film Guide* he bought at a library sale—the guide he used to track what he watched (and to help him decide what to see next) in his early days. Like a good film fan, Michael even did his time working in a video store. Since 2000, he has written for numerous online outlets, most recently the indie film site WayTooIndie.com. In 2014, he founded the MOT Film Society, where he brings classic films to the big screens of Middletown, often to help raise money for charity.

Michael is married with two daughters. This is his first book (but not his first story).

www.ingramcontent.com/pod-product-compliance
Lightning Source LLC
Chambersburg PA
CBHW040303170426
43194CB00021B/2878